History of Law

Foundations and Frameworks Series

From Ancient Codes to Modern Justice: The Evolution of Legal Systems

Adrian Corwin

TME Press email: support@tme.net

Introduction

In 1901, a French team digging in what is now Iran pulled a seven-foot pillar of black stone out of the ground. Carved into it, top to bottom, were nearly 300 laws written almost 4,000 years ago. This was the Code of Hammurabi, and it set out specific rules for trade, marriage, theft, debt, and punishment. One law fixed the wages a builder could charge. Another spelled out what happened if that builder's work collapsed and killed someone. People living in Babylon could walk up to that pillar, read the rules, and know where they stood.

That stone, now displayed in the Louvre, tells us something important. The desire to write down rules, to make them public, and to apply them to everyone is very old. Long before courtrooms, lawyers, and constitutions, humans were already trying to answer the same questions we wrestle with today. What counts as fair? Who decides? What should happen when someone breaks the rules? The answers have changed enormously over the centuries, but the questions have stayed remarkably constant.

This book traces how law developed from those early carved tablets all the way to the complex legal systems that govern us now. It is a story that runs through ancient riverside cities, Greek assemblies, Roman courts, medieval villages, revolutionary parliaments, and modern international tribunals. Along the way you will meet the people, ideas, and turning points that shaped how billions of us live today, often without realizing where any of it came from.

Why the history of law is worth your time

You might think legal history is a dry subject reserved for law students and academics. It is not. The rules you live under every day, the right to a fair trial, the idea that the government itself must follow the law, the protection of private property, the notion that you are innocent until proven guilty, all of these came from somewhere. They were fought over, written down, lost, rediscovered, and refined across thousands of years.

Understanding that history changes how you see the present. When you know that the Magna Carta forced an English king to accept limits on his own power in 1215, modern debates about government authority look different. When you learn that

Roman lawyers worked out detailed rules about contracts and property two thousand years ago, you start to recognize their fingerprints in the agreements you sign today. Legal history is not a museum. It is the foundation under your feet.

There is also a practical payoff. Law shapes business, politics, family life, and international relations. Knowing how legal systems formed helps you understand why different countries handle the same problem in completely different ways. It explains why a contract dispute might be settled one way in France and another way in the United States. It gives you a sharper sense of how power, justice, and order actually work in the real world.

How this book is organized

The book moves in a clear line from the earliest human societies to the present day. Each chapter builds on the one before it, so the ideas accumulate as you read. You don't need any background in law to follow along. Everything is explained in plain language, with real examples wherever possible.

The first chapter looks at law before writing even existed, when small groups settled disputes through custom, kinship, and ritual. From there, the book moves into the first written legal codes, including Hammurabi's famous pillar and the lesser-known codes that came before it.

The middle chapters cover the great legal traditions of the ancient and medieval world. You will explore law in ancient Greece, where Athens experimented with citizen juries and public trials. You will spend time with Roman law, which created structures so durable that they still shape legal systems across Europe and Latin America today. The book also looks beyond the West, examining legal thought in ancient India and China, the development of Islamic law, and the systems that governed the medieval Near East and Asia.

Later chapters trace the slow rise of the English common law, the role of the Church in medieval Europe, and the dramatic legal revolutions of the 1600s and 1700s. This is where ideas about natural rights, the social contract, and the separation of powers took hold, feeding directly into the American Constitution and the Napoleonic Code.

The final chapter brings everything into the modern era. It compares the two great legal families that dominate the world today, civil law and common law. It covers the birth of international law, the rise of human rights, the prosecution of war crimes, and the new challenges that technology is creating for legal systems built long before anyone imagined the internet.

After the main chapters, you will find three closing sections. The Conclusion ties the threads together and reflects on what the long history of law tells us about justice and human society. The Terms and Definitions section gives you a quick reference for the key legal vocabulary used throughout the book, so you never feel lost. The Works Cited and Recommended Readings section points you toward the best sources if you want to go deeper on any topic.

What you will take away

By the end of this book, you will understand the major legal traditions that shaped the modern world and how they connect to one another. You will see how the same basic problems, crime, debt, property, marriage, power, kept reappearing across different societies, and how each one came up with its own answers.

You'll be able to trace specific modern ideas back to their origins. The right to a fair trial, the limits on government power, the protection of contracts, the concept of human rights, all of these have long histories that this book lays out clearly. You will also gain a sense of how legal systems differ around the world today and why those differences exist.

Most of all, you'll come away with a richer understanding of one of humanity's oldest and most important inventions. Law is how societies try to replace violence with order, and chaos with fairness. It's imperfect, it has often been used to protect the powerful at the expense of the weak, and it's still changing. But the long effort to build it, to write down rules and hold everyone to them, is one of the more remarkable things our species has done.

That black stone pulled from the ground in 1901 was just the beginning of a story that is still being written. This book will show you how we got from there to here, and it will give you the background to understand where law might be heading next.

Our first chapter begins where it all started, in the earliest human communities, long before anyone thought to carve a single word into stone.

Outline

Chapter 1: The Origins of Law in Early Human Societies

- Pre-literate legal customs and oral traditions
- Kinship-based dispute resolution in tribal societies
- The role of religion and ritual in early rule-making
- Revenge, restitution, and the first concepts of justice
- The transition from custom to codified rule

Chapter 2: The First Written Legal Codes

- The Code of Ur-Nammu (c. 2100 BCE)
- Hammurabi's Code: structure, penalties, and social hierarchy
- Egyptian Ma'at and royal decree as law
- The Hittite Laws and early contract principles
- The Mosaic Law and its civil applications

Chapter 3: Law in Ancient Greece

- The reforms of Draco and Solon in Athens
- The Athenian jury system and public trials
- Plato and Aristotle on justice and governance
- Natural law theory in Greek philosophy

Chapter 4: Roman Law and Its Lasting Structure

- The Twelve Tables and early Roman codification
- The development of the Roman legal profession
- Justinian's Corpus Juris Civilis
- Roman concepts of property, contract, and tort
- The spread of Roman law across conquered territories

Chapter 5: Law in the Ancient Near East and Asia

- Assyrian law and its treatment of women and property
- Arthashastra: statecraft and law in ancient India
- Legalism versus Confucianism in early Chinese legal thought
- The Laws of Manu and caste-based legal obligation

Chapter 6: Medieval European Legal Systems

- Canon law and the authority of the Catholic Church
- Feudal law and the obligations of lords and serfs
- The Magna Carta (1215) and limits on royal power
- The development of common law courts in England

Chapter 7: Islamic Law and Its Development

- The Quran and Hadith as sources of legal authority
- The four major schools of Sunni jurisprudence
- Sharia in commercial, family, and criminal law
- The role of the qadi in adjudicating disputes
- Islamic law's influence on medieval trade and contract

Chapter 8: The Rise of Common Law and Equity

- Henry II's court reforms and the emergence of common law
- Precedent, stare decisis, and the role of judges
- Courts of Chancery and the origins of equity
- The Statute of Westminster and early parliamentary legislation

Chapter 9: Legal Revolutions of the 17th and 18th Centuries

- Hobbes, Locke, and Rousseau on law and the social contract
- The English Bill of Rights (1689)
- The U.S. Constitution and the separation of powers
- The French Revolution and the Napoleonic Code
- Natural rights theory and its effect on legal reform

Chapter 10: Modern Legal Systems and International Law

- Civil law versus common law systems today
- The formation of international law from Westphalia to the UN
- Human rights law and the Universal Declaration (1948)
- The International Criminal Court and war crimes prosecution
- Emerging challenges: digital law, AI regulation, and cross-border jurisdiction

Conclusion

Example Answers to End-of-Chapter Questions

General Timeline of Legal History

Terms and Definitions

Works Cited & Recommended Readings

Contents

Chapter 1: The Origins of Law in Early Human Societies

Picture a small band of humans huddled around a fire roughly forty thousand years ago. Two of them are arguing. One accuses the other of taking meat that wasn't his to take. Voices rise. Others in the group stop what they're doing and watch. There are no police here, no judges, no written rules posted on a wall. And yet something has to happen next, because the group cannot afford to let this fester. If the two men come to blows, the whole band is weaker. If the theft goes unanswered, others might start taking whatever they please.

What happens in that moment, around that fire, is law. Not law as we'd recognize it in a courtroom, but law in its rawest and most essential form. A dispute arises. The group has to deal with it. Some shared sense of what's right and what isn't gets applied. A resolution follows, and life goes on. This basic sequence has repeated itself billions of times across human history, and it was happening long before anyone thought to write a single word down.

We tend to assume law began with writing, with codes carved into stone and statutes recorded on clay. But those written codes came late in the story. By the time Hammurabi's scribes were pressing rules into wet clay, humans had already been living under law for tens of thousands of years. The written codes didn't invent law. They wrote down something that already existed, something people had been practicing for a very long time. This chapter is about that older law, the law that governed human life before the first word was ever recorded.

Pre-literate legal customs and oral traditions

For roughly 95 percent of human existence, there was no writing. Anatomically modern humans have been around for at least 200,000 years, and the first written legal codes appear only about 4,000 years ago. That leaves an enormous stretch of time, thousands of generations, during which people lived, argued, cooperated, and settled conflicts without any written rules at all. And they managed it. Human societies didn't descend into constant violence. They developed intricate systems of custom and expectation that told everyone how to behave and what to do when someone stepped out of line.

These systems were carried entirely in memory and speech. This is what we mean by oral tradition. The rules lived in people's heads and passed from one generation to the next through storytelling, instruction, ritual, and repetition. A child growing up in such a society learned the rules the same way they learned language, by absorbing them from the people around them, day after day, until the rules felt as natural and obvious as breathing.

We know a great deal about how this worked because oral legal traditions survived into recent history, and in many places they still operate today. Anthropologists who lived among societies without writing recorded in detail how these systems functioned. What they found overturns the old assumption that people without written law lived in chaos. The opposite was true. Many of these societies had legal customs more detailed, more nuanced, and more strictly observed than anything in a modern legal textbook.

Consider the customary law of many Indigenous Australian communities, which stretches back tens of thousands of years and represents one of the longest continuous legal traditions on Earth. Their law governed marriage, land use, ritual obligations, punishment for wrongdoing, and the relationships between different groups. None of it was written. It was held in songs, stories, ceremonies, and the memories of elders, and it regulated behavior with remarkable precision. A person knew whom they could marry, who had rights to hunt in which territory, what was owed when an offense occurred, and what would happen if obligations went unmet. These weren't vague notions. They were specific, binding rules that people followed because everyone around them followed them too.

Oral law had real advantages that we sometimes overlook because we're so used to writing. It was flexible. A written rule sits frozen on the page, and changing it requires a formal process. An oral rule can adapt gradually as circumstances shift, without anyone needing to formally amend anything. The custom simply evolves as elders reinterpret it and pass along the updated version. This let pre-literate legal systems respond to change in ways that were fluid and organic.

But oral law also had a serious weakness, and it's the reason writing eventually became so important. Memory is fallible, and it varies from person to person. Two elders might genuinely remember a rule differently. Over generations, customs could drift, and there was no fixed reference point to check them against. When a dispute turned on exactly what the rule was, the answer depended on whose memory the group trusted. This created room for uncertainty and manipulation. A powerful person might "remember" a rule in a way that happened to benefit them. Without a written text to appeal to, resolving these disagreements meant relying on the authority and reputation of whoever was doing the remembering.

To manage this weakness, oral societies developed techniques for preserving their rules accurately. Repetition was central. Rules were often embedded in verse, song, or rhythmic sayings, because structured language is far easier to memorize precisely than ordinary prose. Rhyme and meter act as error-correction, since a mistake breaks the pattern and gets noticed. Proverbs served a similar function, compressing a legal principle into a short, memorable phrase that could be recited and applied. A saying like "the one who kindles the fire is responsible for the burn" packs a rule about liability into a form that sticks in the mind and passes easily from person to person.

Specialists also emerged. In many societies, certain people held the role of remembering and reciting the law. They trained for years to memorize vast bodies of custom, genealogy, and precedent. Among some West African peoples, the griot filled a role like this, serving as a living archive of history, lineage, and law. When a dispute arose that touched on precedent or inherited obligation, the community turned to these human libraries. Their memory was the closest thing the society had to a legal record, and their reliability was essential to keeping the whole system functioning.

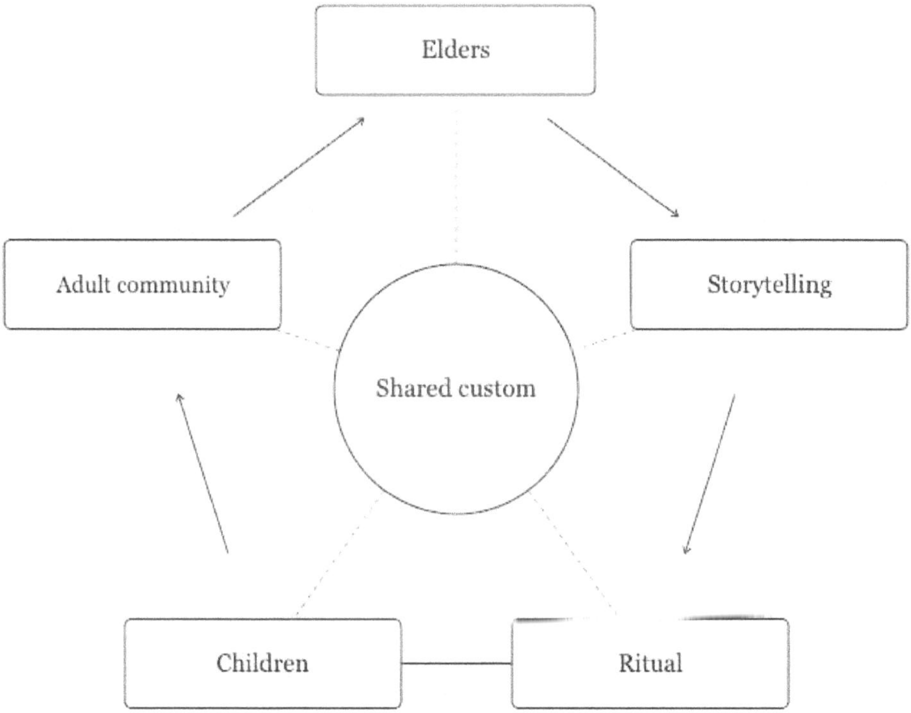

Kinship-based dispute resolution in tribal societies

In societies without formal states, courts, or police, one question towers over all others when a conflict breaks out: who are you related to? Kinship was the organizing principle of early human society, and it was also the backbone of how disputes got resolved. Your family, your clan, your lineage, these weren't just sources of affection and belonging. They were your legal support system, your protection, and, when necessary, your enforcement mechanism.

Understanding this requires setting aside the modern idea that legal disputes happen between individuals. In much of human history, disputes weren't really between individuals at all. They were between groups. If a man from one clan injured a man from another, it wasn't simply a matter between those two men. It became a matter between their two clans. The injured man's relatives took up his cause, and the offender's relatives stood behind him. Conflict resolution meant negotiation between these groups, not a proceeding involving two isolated individuals.

This group-based structure shaped everything about how justice worked. Responsibility was collective. If you committed an offense, your entire kin group might be held liable for it, and any of them might be called on to pay compensation or face retaliation. This sounds harsh to modern ears, but it served an important function. It gave every family a powerful stake in keeping its own members in line. If your cousin's bad behavior could cost you cattle or put you in danger, you had every reason to make sure your cousin behaved. The kin group policed itself, because the whole group bore the consequences of any member's actions. This was a form of social control that worked without any central authority at all.

The strength of your kin group determined your security and your standing. A person from a large, powerful clan enjoyed real protection, because anyone who wronged them knew they'd face the anger of many relatives. A person with few relatives, or one who'd been cast out by their family, was dangerously exposed. To lose the backing of your kin was to lose your legal protection entirely, which is why exile or expulsion from the group ranked among the most severe punishments a society could impose. A person without kin had no one to avenge them, no one to negotiate on their behalf, and no one to pay compensation for their protection. They were, in the fullest sense, an outlaw, standing outside the law's protection.

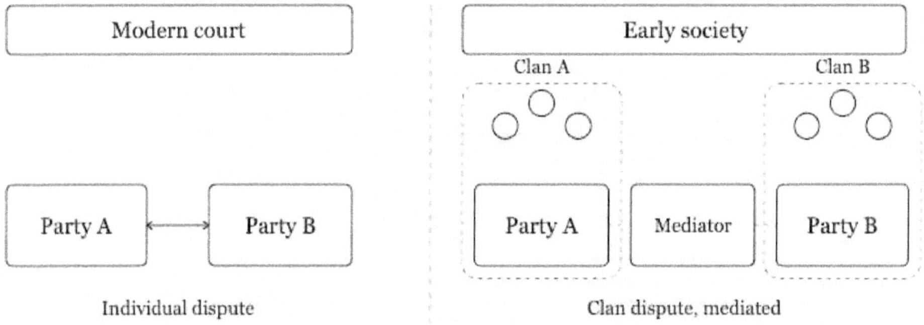

Marriage and the exchange of goods were deeply tied to this legal structure. When two people married, it often created a formal alliance between their families, complete with obligations that both sides were expected to honor. Bridewealth, the transfer of goods from the groom's family to the bride's, wasn't a purchase of the bride, as it's sometimes misunderstood. It functioned as a legal instrument that bound the two families together and established mutual obligations. It compensated the bride's family for the loss of her labor and children to her husband's group, and it created a stake that discouraged mistreatment, since a wronged wife might return to her family and the bridewealth might have to be repaid. These exchanges knitted families into webs of obligation that stabilized the wider society.

Because disputes could escalate into dangerous feuds between kin groups, most societies developed methods for cooling conflicts down before they spiraled. Mediation was common, and it usually relied on neutral third parties who were respected by both sides. Sometimes these were elders whose age and reputation gave them the standing to broker a settlement. Sometimes they were people connected to both groups through marriage, who had an interest in keeping the peace. The mediator's job wasn't to issue a verdict and impose it by force, since they typically had no force to impose anything. Their job was to guide the two sides toward an agreement both could accept, one that satisfied the injured party enough to prevent revenge while not humiliating the offender's group so badly that they'd resist.

This points to something important about early law that's easy to miss. In the absence of a central authority that could enforce decisions, the goal of dispute resolution wasn't always to determine guilt and mete out punishment in the way a modern court does.

Often the real goal was to restore peace between groups and prevent the conflict from tearing the community apart. A settlement that both sides accepted, even if it didn't perfectly reflect who was right and who was wrong, was better than an ongoing feud that could kill people on both sides for years. This practical emphasis on restoring social harmony, rather than on abstract justice, ran through much of pre-state law.

The Nuer people of what's now South Sudan offer a well-documented example of how this worked. When a killing occurred, it created a blood feud between the kin groups of the killer and the victim, and this feud carried a genuine threat of retaliatory violence. To resolve it, a religious figure called the Leopard-Skin Chief would step in as a neutral mediator. He held no power to command anyone, but his ritual status let him offer sanctuary to a killer and pressure both sides toward a settlement, usually involving the payment of cattle to compensate the victim's family. The system worked not because anyone could enforce it, but because both sides understood that the alternative, an endless cycle of revenge killings, was worse for everyone.

The role of religion and ritual in early rule making

Where did early law get its authority? A modern law carries force because the state stands behind it, with courts to interpret it and police to enforce it. But early societies had no state. So what made people obey rules when there was no government to compel them? A large part of the answer is religion. In the earliest human societies, law and religion weren't separate things. They were woven together so tightly that the distinction we draw between them today would have made little sense.

The rules that governed behavior were commonly understood as sacred, handed down by ancestors, spirits, or gods rather than invented by people. This gave law a weight and permanence that purely human rules could never have. If a rule came from a mortal, someone might reasonably ask why they should obey it, and might defy it if they thought they could get away with doing so. But if a rule came from the gods or the ancestors, defying it meant risking supernatural punishment, and that was a far more frightening prospect than any human penalty. A person might escape their neighbors' notice, but they couldn't hide from the spirits.

This sacred quality solved the enforcement problem in a society without police. When people believe that breaking a rule will bring sickness, crop failure, misfortune, or the anger of the dead, they police themselves out of genuine fear. The threat doesn't require anyone to catch you in the act. The gods already know. This internalized sense of religious obligation was one of the most effective enforcement mechanisms early societies had, precisely because it operated inside each person's own mind, everywhere and at all times, without any need for external watchmen.

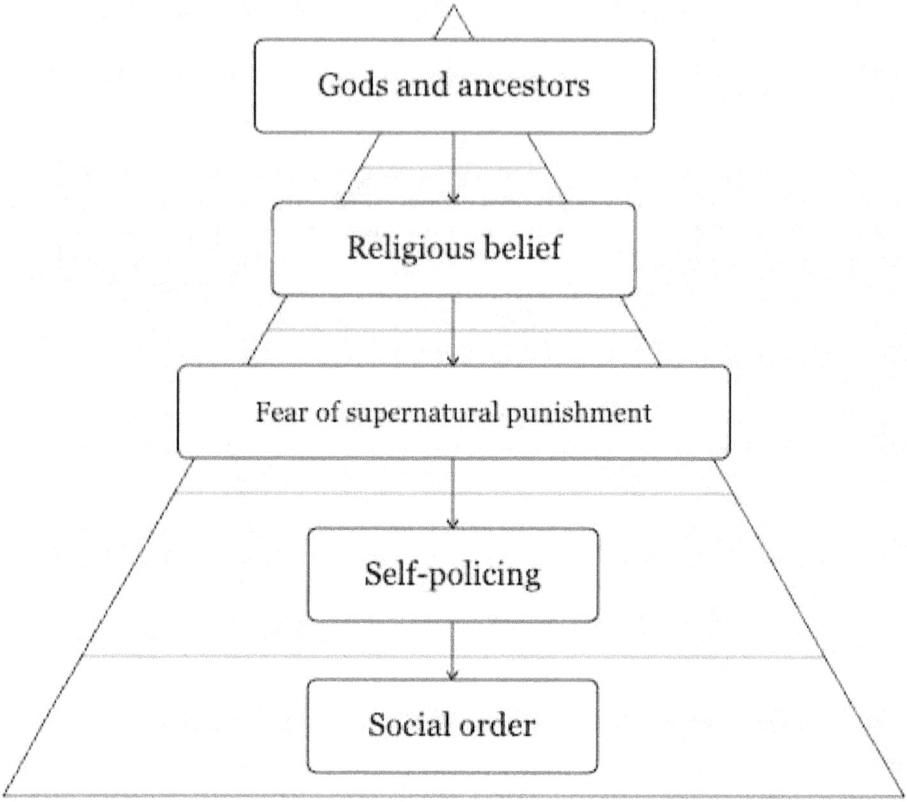

Rituals gave law its visible form in societies that had no written texts to consult. A ritual is a formal, repeated set of actions performed in a prescribed way, and it did several kinds of legal work at once. Rituals marked important transitions and made them official. A marriage became real and binding through the performance of the correct ceremony, which announced the new relationship to the community and to the spirits, establishing the obligations that came with it. Without the ritual, there was no marriage. The ceremony was the legal act itself, not a mere celebration of something that had already happened.

The oath was one of the most important legal rituals of all, and versions of it survive in courtrooms to this day. To swear an oath was to call on the gods to witness your words and to invite their punishment if you lied. In a society without documents, without recordings, and without reliable ways to verify claims, the oath was a technology for producing truth. A person who swore falsely wasn't just risking their reputation among neighbors. They were inviting divine wrath onto themselves and possibly their whole family. The fear of that consequence was often enough to make people tell the truth when it mattered, or to keep quiet if they couldn't. When we make witnesses swear to tell the truth today, we're performing a faded version of a ritual that once carried terrifying supernatural weight.

Ordeals and divination were used to settle disputes that ordinary evidence couldn't resolve. When there was no way to know who was telling the truth, some societies turned the question over to the gods through an ordeal. An accused person might be made to grasp a hot iron, plunge a hand into boiling water, or ingest a poison, and their guilt or innocence would be read from the result. The belief was that the gods would protect the innocent and let the guilty suffer.

To us this seems like a cruel and irrational way to determine guilt, and by any evidentiary standard it was. But it made sense within a worldview where the divine was understood to intervene directly in human affairs, and it served a practical function: it provided a way to reach a final, accepted decision in cases that would otherwise have no resolution and might drag on to violence. Once the ordeal had spoken, the matter was closed, because arguing with the outcome meant arguing with the gods.

Divination worked on a similar principle. Rather than testing an accused person's body, it read the will of the gods from signs: the pattern of thrown bones, the markings on an animal's liver, the flight of birds. Specialists trained to interpret these signs would deliver the verdict. In many societies these religious specialists, the priests, shamans, and diviners, were among the most important legal authorities, precisely because they were understood to have access to the divine knowledge that ordinary people lacked. Their role blended the religious and the legal so completely that separating the two would have been meaningless. To interpret the will of the gods was to declare the law.

Revenge, restitution, and the first concepts of justice

At the heart of every legal system, ancient or modern, sits a hard question: what should happen when someone does wrong? The earliest and most instinctive answer was revenge. When someone harms you or your kin, you harm them back. This impulse runs deep in human nature, and it appears in some form in nearly every early society. It also appears in nearly every human being, which is why we still feel its pull when we're wronged, even though we live under systems designed to take revenge out of our hands.

Revenge served a genuine purpose in societies without any central authority to punish wrongdoing. If there's no state to deter crime, the threat of retaliation from a victim's kin becomes the main thing standing between order and chaos. A person contemplating theft or violence had to weigh the near-certainty that the victim's relatives would strike back. In this sense, the threat of revenge functioned as a crude but real deterrent, holding behavior in check where no other enforcement existed. The knowledge that harming someone would bring their whole family down on you kept a great deal of harm from happening in the first place.

But revenge carried a terrible danger. Once it began, it could spiral without end. My kin group harms yours, so yours harms mine back, and each act of retaliation becomes a fresh injury demanding its own response. This is the blood feud, and it could poison relations between groups for generations, killing people who had nothing to do with the original offense. A feud that started with a single insult or a single death could consume dozens of lives over decades. Every early society that relied on revenge faced this problem, and much of the development of early law can be understood as an effort to contain the destructive potential of vengeance while preserving its deterrent value.

The first great innovation was the limiting principle, the idea that revenge, if taken, must be proportionate to the original harm. This is the true meaning of the famous phrase "an eye for an eye," which people today often misread as a call for harsh, brutal punishment. It's the opposite. The principle set a ceiling, not a floor. It declared that if someone took your eye, you could take one eye in return, and no more. You couldn't kill them for it, and you couldn't wipe out their family. In a world where a minor injury might otherwise trigger a killing, and a killing might trigger a massacre, the rule of exact proportionality was a profound restraint on violence. It capped retaliation at the level of the original offense and, in doing so, kept feuds from escalating beyond all reason.

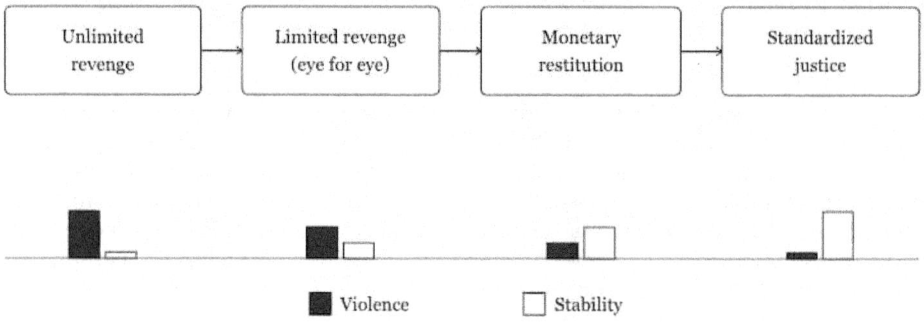

The second great innovation went further and changed the course of legal history: the replacement of revenge with payment. Instead of taking an eye for an eye, why not accept goods, livestock, or valuables as compensation for the injury? This idea, that a wrong could be settled by a transfer of wealth rather than by retaliation, is one of the most important developments in the entire history of law. It's the principle of restitution, and it offered a way out of the cycle of violence that revenge created. The victim's kin received compensation for their loss. The offender's kin paid a price but kept their lives and their blood. And the feud was resolved without anyone else having to die.

Systems of compensation became remarkably detailed. Many societies developed precise schedules assigning a specific value to specific injuries, so that everyone knew in advance what a particular wrong would cost. The loss of a hand was worth so much, an eye so much, a front tooth some lesser amount, and a life the highest sum of all. The early Germanic legal traditions of medieval Europe formalized this into a system called wergild, literally "man-price," which set the compensation owed for killing a person according to their rank and status in society. A nobleman's life carried a far higher wergild than a commoner's, which tells us plainly that these early systems reflected and reinforced social hierarchy rather than treating everyone as equal. Justice wasn't blind. It could see exactly who you were, and it priced your life accordingly.

These compensation schedules represent something genuinely new in human thought: an attempt to make justice predictable and consistent. When the price of a wrong is fixed and known in advance, disputes become easier to settle, because both sides already know roughly what the outcome should be. There's less to argue about. The schedule also curbs the discretion of whoever is judging the dispute, since they can't simply invent a penalty on the spot but must apply the established rate. In this move toward fixed, knowable consequences, we can see the early stirrings of something we'd recognize as the rule of law: the notion that like cases should be treated alike, and that the response to a wrong should follow a rule rather than a whim.

The table below lays out the progression from raw revenge to structured restitution, showing how each stage tackled the weaknesses of the one before it.

Stage	Core Principle	Problem It Solved	Weakness That Remained
Unlimited revenge	Harm answered with harm	Deterred wrongdoing where no authority existed	Feuds escalated without end
Proportionate revenge	Retaliation capped at the level of the offense	Prevented minor wrongs from triggering massacres	Still relied on violence and left both sides injured
Restitution	Wrongs settled by payment of goods	Ended feuds without bloodshed	Priced justice by status, favoring the powerful
Fixed compensation schedules	Set values assigned to specific wrongs	Made outcomes predictable and consistent	Entrenched existing social hierarchy

Running through all of this is a slowly developing idea of justice itself. At first, justice meant little more than getting even, restoring the balance that a wrong had upset. But as compensation systems grew more elaborate, a richer notion began to emerge: that there was a right amount owed for a given wrong, a correct response that existed independently of what any particular victim happened to want. This is the seed of an idea that would grow for thousands of years, the idea that justice is something more than personal satisfaction, that it involves a standard outside the individuals in dispute, a measure of what's owed that everyone can appeal to. That seed was planted in these early systems of revenge and restitution, long before anyone had the words to describe what they were reaching toward.

The transition from custom to codified rule

For most of human history, law lived in memory and speech. Then, gradually, in a handful of places around the world, people began writing it down. This shift, from unwritten custom to written code, ranks among the most consequential developments in the history of law. It didn't happen everywhere, and where it did happen, it happened slowly and for particular reasons. Understanding why some societies made this move, and what changed when they did, sets the stage for everything that follows in this book.

Writing law down required writing itself, and writing was invented independently only a few times in human history, most notably in Mesopotamia around 3200 BCE. It's no accident that the world's earliest known written laws come from the same region that produced the world's earliest writing. But the invention of writing didn't immediately produce written law. For centuries, people used writing mainly for keeping records of goods, taxes, and trade, the practical business of managing an economy. Only later did it occur to anyone to use this new technology to record the rules a society lived by. The gap between the invention of writing and its application to law tells us that writing law down wasn't obvious. It was a step that had to be discovered, and it answered needs that only arose under particular conditions.

Those conditions had to do with scale and complexity. As long as people lived in small groups where everyone knew everyone else, oral custom worked well enough. The rules were known to all, disputes were rare among familiar faces, and respected elders could settle whatever conflicts arose. But as societies grew larger, this began to break down. Cities brought together thousands of strangers who shared no common upbringing and no personal bonds of trust. Trade linked distant communities with different customs. Kings ruled over populations far too large to govern through personal relationships alone. In these conditions, the old system of unwritten custom held in the memories of elders started to strain. It couldn't reliably coordinate the behavior of masses of people who didn't know one another and couldn't agree on what the customs even were.

Written law addressed these strains in several ways. It created a fixed, public reference point that anyone could appeal to, ending the uncertainty that came when rules lived only in fallible and inconsistent memories. It let rulers project authority across a wide territory, since a written decree could travel to distant provinces and be applied uniformly in places the ruler would never personally visit. And it brought a new consistency to the administration of justice, since officials in different cities could apply the same written rules rather than each relying on their own recollection of local custom. Writing turned law into something that could hold together a large and diverse society in a way that oral tradition never could.

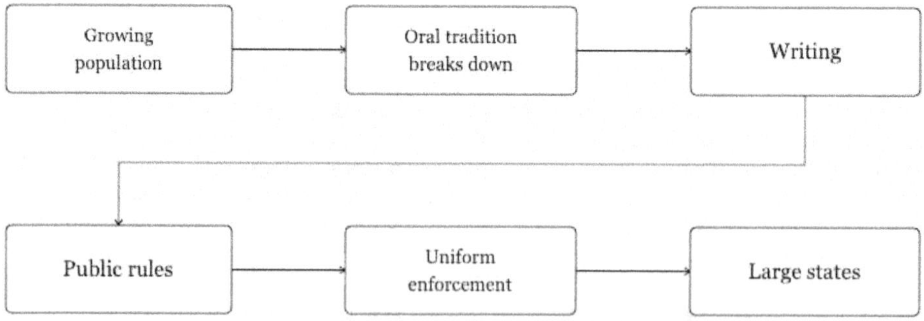

There was also a political dimension to writing law down, and it cut in two directions at once. On one hand, a written code was a tool of royal power, letting a king impose his will across his realm and monument his authority in permanent form. When Hammurabi had his laws carved onto a towering stone pillar and set up in public, he was making a statement about his own greatness and his role as the source of justice for his people. The code advertised his power as much as it regulated behavior.

On the other hand, writing law down also placed a subtle limit on that very power. Once a rule is written and made public, it becomes harder for a ruler to simply ignore it or change it at whim, because everyone can see what the rule is and hold the ruler to it. A written law commits its author to something. It becomes a standard that even the powerful can be measured against. This tension, between written law as an instrument of authority and written law as a constraint on authority, runs through the entire history of law from these earliest codes onward. It's a tension we're still living with today, and it began the moment the first ruler decided to make the rules public.

It's worth being clear about what these earliest written codes actually were and weren't, because it's easy to misunderstand them. They weren't comprehensive legal systems that covered every situation, the way a modern legal code aspires to do. They tended to be collections of specific rulings and provisions addressing particular problems: what to do about a certain kind of theft, how to handle a certain dispute over property, what compensation was owed for a certain injury. Much of the actual law of these societies remained unwritten custom, and the written codes sat on top of that deeper foundation rather than replacing it. The code was a supplement to custom, addressing selected matters that seemed to need the clarity and authority of a written statement, while the vast body of everyday law continued to live, as it always had, in the unwritten practices of the people.

We should also resist imagining that written law swept away oral tradition in a single stroke. The two coexisted for a very long time, and in much of the world unwritten custom remained the primary form of law for thousands of years after writing appeared. Even in societies with sophisticated written codes, ordinary people often continued to settle their disputes through customary means, mediation by elders, negotiation between kin groups, the same methods humans had always used. Written law and oral custom weren't rival systems where one had to defeat the other. They were layers, operating side by side, each handling the kinds of matters it was suited to. The written code addressed the concerns of the state and the marketplace, while custom continued to govern the intimate business of family, kin, and local community.

What the move to writing set in motion was a long, slow, uneven process by which more and more of human law came to be recorded, systematized, and administered through written texts. That process is still going on. But it began here, in the transition from custom to code, when a few societies faced with the challenge of governing large and complex populations reached for a new technology and used it to fix their rules in permanent, public form. Everything that comes later in the history of law, the great codes of the ancient world, the legal systems of Greece and Rome, the traditions that shaped the modern world, grows out of this first decisive step from the remembered rule to the written one.

Discussion question: If unwritten custom governed human societies successfully for tens of thousands of years, and written law brought both greater consistency and new forms of power over ordinary people, can we really say the shift to written law was progress? Or did societies gain something and lose something at the same time, and if so, what exactly did they trade away?

Chapter 2: The First Written Legal Codes

Around 1750 BCE, a stonecutter in Babylon spent weeks carving nearly 300 laws into a slab of black diorite taller than a person. At the top, an image showed King Hammurabi standing before the sun god, receiving the authority to rule. Below it, in dense columns of cuneiform script, ran the rules: what happened if you struck your father, what a surgeon could charge, what was owed when an ox gored a man in the street. The finished pillar stood in a public place for anyone to see, a permanent monument to the king's justice and a warning to anyone who might disturb it.

That pillar survives today in the Louvre in Paris, and it's the most famous legal artifact from the ancient world. But it wasn't the first. By the time Hammurabi's laws were carved, written legal codes had existed in Mesopotamia for over three centuries.

Other peoples, in other places, were developing their own written laws too, each shaped by its own society, its own gods, and its own idea of what justice required. This chapter looks at the earliest of these written codes, the documents that first fixed human law in permanent form, and at what they reveal about the societies that produced them.

Reading these ancient codes is like looking through a window into worlds that vanished thousands of years ago. They tell us what people valued and feared, how they organized their societies, whom they protected and whom they didn't, and what they thought justice meant. They're among the oldest written documents we have, and they show us that the questions we still wrestle with, about fairness, punishment, property, and power, were already being wrestled with at the very dawn of recorded history.

The Code of Ur-Nammu (c. 2100 BCE)

The oldest surviving law code in the world doesn't belong to Hammurabi. It belongs to a king named Ur-Nammu, who ruled the Sumerian city of Ur roughly 350 years before Hammurabi carved his famous pillar. The Code of Ur-Nammu dates to around 2100 BCE, and though it survives only in fragments copied onto clay tablets, those fragments are enough to reveal a legal system already sophisticated in ways that overturn our assumptions about how "primitive" the earliest law must have been.

Ur-Nammu founded the Third Dynasty of Ur, a Sumerian state that controlled much of southern Mesopotamia. Whether the code bears his name because he personally commissioned it or because it was issued under his son Shulgi remains uncertain, since the historical record from four thousand years ago is inevitably patchy. What isn't uncertain is the significance of the document itself. Written in Sumerian, it predates Hammurabi's Babylonian code by centuries and stands as the earliest written law humanity has yet recovered.

The code opens with a prologue, and this prologue is worth pausing on, because it establishes a pattern that would echo through ancient law for the next two thousand years. In it, the king presents himself as chosen by the gods to bring justice to the land, and he describes the reforms he carried out. He claims to have established honest weights and measures, to have protected the vulnerable, and to have ensured that the orphan didn't fall prey to the wealthy, that the widow didn't fall prey to the powerful, that the man of one shekel didn't fall prey to the man of one mina. This image, of the king as a shepherd defending the weak against the strong, became the standard way ancient rulers justified their authority, and Ur-Nammu is the earliest ruler we can see making the claim in writing.

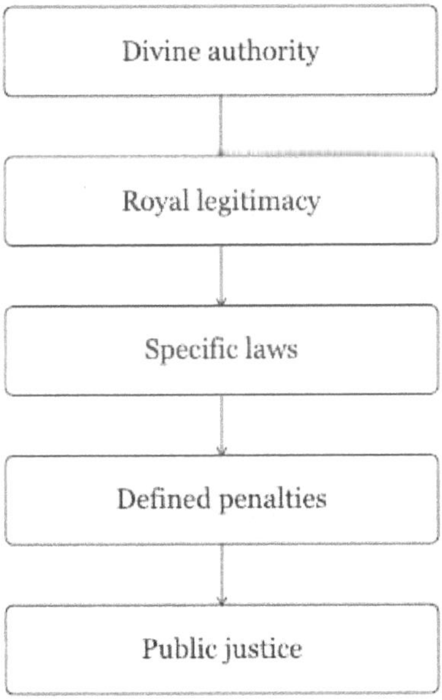

The most striking feature of the code is how it punished wrongdoing, because it differs sharply from what came later. The Code of Ur-Nammu relied heavily on monetary compensation for physical injuries. If a man cut off another man's foot, he paid ten shekels of silver. If he broke a man's bone with a weapon, he paid one mina of silver. If he cut off another man's nose, he paid two-thirds of a mina. This is restitution, the settling of wrongs by payment rather than by retaliation, written into law with specific amounts attached to specific injuries.

The contrast with Hammurabi's later code is dramatic and revealing. Where Ur-Nammu prescribed a silver payment for a bodily injury, Hammurabi, centuries later, prescribed physical retaliation, the eye for an eye. This is the opposite of what we might expect. We tend to assume law grows steadily gentler over time, moving from brutal physical punishment toward more civilized monetary penalties. Yet here the older code is the more monetary one, and the later code is the more physically retaliatory. The history of law doesn't march in a straight line from cruelty to mercy. It zigzags, shaped by the particular values and circumstances of each society, and Ur-Nammu's code is the evidence that even the very earliest written law could take an approach that strikes us as surprisingly measured.

Not every offense in Ur-Nammu's code was handled by payment. The code reserved the death penalty for a small number of serious crimes, including murder, robbery, and certain sexual offenses. A man who committed murder was to be killed. A man who deflowered another man's virgin wife was to be killed. So the code wasn't uniformly lenient, and it drew a line between offenses grave enough to demand death and lesser wrongs that money could settle. But the general reliance on compensation for physical injury marks it out and tells us that the principle of restitution, which we saw emerging in unwritten custom, had by this point been formalized into written law with a precision that left little room for dispute.

The code also addressed matters well beyond injury and violence. It contained provisions on marriage and divorce, setting out what a man owed if he divorced his first wife and what he owed if he divorced a widow he'd married. It dealt with false accusations, prescribing penalties for those who accused others of crimes they couldn't prove. It touched on the return of runaway slaves and the rewards owed to those who brought them back, a reminder that these were slaveholding societies whose law took the institution of slavery entirely for granted. And it addressed agricultural disputes, the practical conflicts over land, water, and crops that were the daily stuff of life in a farming society dependent on the flooding of the Tigris and Euphrates.

What the Code of Ur-Nammu shows us, above all, is that written law arrived on the scene already mature. This wasn't a crude first attempt, a society fumbling toward the idea of written rules. It was a coherent legal document with a clear structure, a stated philosophy of royal justice, specific and consistent penalties, and coverage of the main areas of social and economic life. The sophistication of the oldest law we possess suggests that the practices behind it, the settling of disputes, the assigning of penalties, the balancing of interests, had been developing for a very long time before anyone thought to write them down. When writing finally captured the law, it captured something already fully formed.

Hammurabi's Code: structure, penalties, and social hierarchy

Hammurabi ruled Babylon from roughly 1792 to 1750 BCE, and over his long reign he transformed a modest city-state into the dominant power of Mesopotamia. But his lasting fame rests less on his conquests than on the code of laws he left behind.

The Code of Hammurabi is the most complete and best-preserved legal document from the ancient Near East, and it has shaped our understanding of early law more than any other single source. Nearly 300 provisions survive intact, carved onto that famous diorite pillar, giving us an unusually full picture of how one ancient society tried to regulate itself.

The code follows a recognizable structure. It opens with a prologue in which Hammurabi, like Ur-Nammu before him, presents himself as chosen by the gods to establish justice and protect the weak from oppression. The body of the code then works through a wide range of subjects: property, trade, debt, family, injury, professional conduct, and agriculture. It closes with an epilogue that calls down elaborate curses on anyone who would deface the monument or ignore its laws, and blessings on any future ruler who upholds them. The whole document is framed as a permanent act of royal justice, meant to endure for all time.

The famous principle running through much of the code is retribution in kind, the idea captured in the phrase "an eye for an eye, a tooth for a tooth." The Latin term for this is lex talionis, the law of retaliation. If a man destroyed the eye of another man, his own eye was to be destroyed. If he broke another man's bone, his bone was to be broken. If he knocked out the tooth of an equal, his own tooth was knocked out. This mirroring of the offense in the punishment is what most people remember about Hammurabi's code, and it represents a philosophy of justice in which the penalty precisely matches the crime.

Here's where the code becomes far more revealing than the simple phrase suggests, because lex talionis didn't apply equally to everyone. Whether you got an eye for an eye depended entirely on who you were and who your victim was. Babylonian society was divided into distinct classes, and the code treated these classes very differently. At the top were the awilum, the free men of property and full legal standing. In the middle were the mushkenum, a class of dependents or commoners of lower status whose exact position scholars still debate. At the bottom were the wardum, the slaves, who were treated in law as property rather than as full persons.

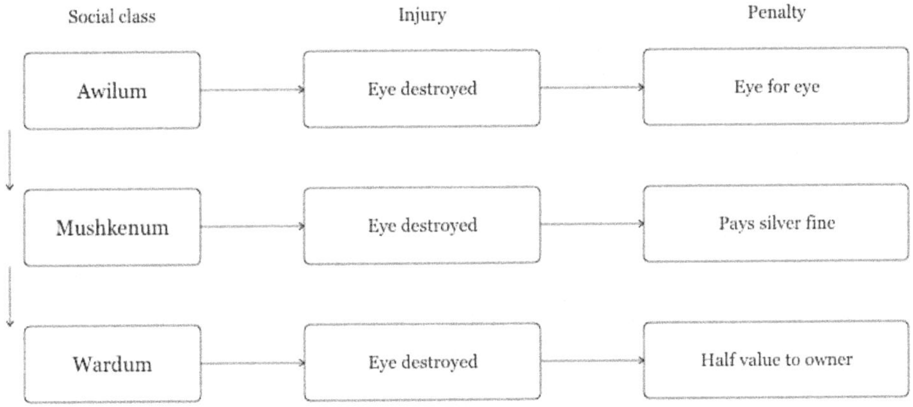

The penalties shifted dramatically along these class lines. If an awilum destroyed the eye of another awilum, his own eye was destroyed, the pure talion of equal against equal. But if an awilum destroyed the eye of a mushkenum, he didn't lose his eye. He simply paid a fine in silver. And if an awilum destroyed the eye of a slave, he paid the slave's owner half the slave's value, because the injury was treated as damage to another man's property, not as harm to a person. The same physical act, the destruction of an eye, carried three completely different consequences depending on the social rank of the victim. Talion in its full, bodily form applied only between social equals. Below that, the law switched to compensation, and the value of the compensation dropped as the victim's status dropped.

This makes something plain that we need to understand about ancient law: it wasn't built on any notion of human equality. The idea that all people deserve equal treatment under the law, which we take as fundamental today, would have been alien to Hammurabi's world. His code openly and explicitly assigned different worth to different classes of people, and it built that inequality into the very structure of its penalties. A person's legal protection depended on their rank. The higher your status, the more the law valued your body, your property, and your word.

The code's treatment of professionals shows the same logic of proportionate, sometimes harsh, consequences. Its provisions on builders are famous and unsettling. If a builder constructed a house so poorly that it collapsed and killed the owner, the builder was to be put to death. If the collapse killed the owner's son, then the builder's son was to be put to death.

This last provision reveals another feature of the code that jars against modern principles: it sometimes punished not the wrongdoer but an innocent member of the wrongdoer's family, treating the family as an extension of the person. The builder's son had done nothing, yet he could pay with his life for his father's shoddy work, because the penalty was designed to mirror the harm exactly, a son for a son.

The code covered an enormous range of everyday economic life, and this practical detail is part of what makes it so valuable to historians. It set the wages of laborers and the fees of surgeons, veterinarians, and boatmen. It regulated the rental of fields and the hiring of oxen. It dealt with the responsibilities of merchants and their agents, the handling of debts, and the taking of deposits. It addressed the conduct of tavern keepers, laid out the rules for irrigation and the liability of a farmer whose neglect of the dikes flooded his neighbor's field, and governed a host of commercial arrangements. Reading these provisions, we see a bustling, complex economy with specialized trades, active commerce, and a legal system trying to bring order to the countless transactions and conflicts that such an economy generated.

Marriage and family occupied a large portion of the code, and here too the provisions reveal the values of the society. Marriage was a contract, and the code specified the obligations of husband and wife, the handling of dowries, the grounds for divorce, and the treatment of children and inheritance. Women had certain protections under the code, including rights to property and provisions that guarded a wife against arbitrary abandonment, and a widow was entitled to keep her dowry and remain in her husband's house. But women were also clearly subordinate to men within the family structure, and the penalties for offenses like adultery fell far more heavily on women than on men. The code offered women real, if limited, legal standing, within a system that remained firmly patriarchal.

The table below shows how the same injury drew different penalties depending on the class of the victim, making visible the graded structure of Babylonian justice.

Offense	Victim's Class	Penalty
Destroying an eye	Awilum (free man)	Offender's own eye destroyed

Destroying an eye	Mushkenum (commoner)	Fine paid in silver
Destroying an eye	Wardum (slave)	Half the slave's value paid to owner
Striking to knock out a tooth	Equal	Offender's own tooth knocked out
Striking a person of higher rank	Superior	Public flogging

The genius of Hammurabi's code, and the reason it mattered so much, lies in what it accomplished for its society regardless of the inequalities baked into it. By publishing a fixed set of penalties, it made the consequences of actions predictable. People could know in advance what a given wrong would cost, which reduced the arbitrariness of justice and limited the discretion of those who judged disputes. A judge couldn't simply invent a penalty; he was supposed to apply the established one. This is a real step toward the rule of law, the principle that legal outcomes should follow known rules rather than the mood or interest of whoever holds power. That the rules themselves were deeply unequal doesn't erase the significance of having public, fixed rules at all. Hammurabi's Babylon still ranked people by class, but it had committed itself, in permanent stone, to a system where the response to a wrong followed a written standard that even the powerful were meant to respect.

Egyptian Ma'at and royal decree as law

Egypt presents a puzzle that sets it apart from its neighbors in Mesopotamia. Here was one of the greatest, most enduring, and most sophisticated civilizations of the ancient world, a state that lasted for three thousand years and built monuments that still stand. Yet from all those centuries, we have no written law code comparable to Hammurabi's. No Egyptian pharaoh, as far as we know, ever carved a comprehensive collection of laws into stone for public display. This absence isn't an accident of preservation, some lost tablet waiting to be found. It reflects a fundamentally different idea about what law was and where it came from.

At the center of the Egyptian understanding of law and order stood a concept called Ma'at. Ma'at is difficult to translate into a single English word because it meant several interconnected things at once: truth, justice, balance, order, harmony, and the proper functioning of the cosmos. Ma'at was the principle that held the universe together, keeping the sun rising, the Nile flooding, and society running as it should. It was personified as a goddess, depicted with a feather on her head, and it represented the natural and moral order that everything, from the movement of the stars to the conduct of human beings, was supposed to follow.

Egyptian law was understood as the expression of Ma'at in human affairs. To act justly was to act in accordance with Ma'at, to uphold the balance and order of the world. To act unjustly was to introduce chaos, to disturb the harmony that Ma'at maintained. This meant law wasn't primarily a set of specific written rules. It was the ongoing effort to keep human society aligned with a cosmic principle of rightness. Justice wasn't about matching a case to a statute; it was about restoring the proper balance that a wrong had upset.

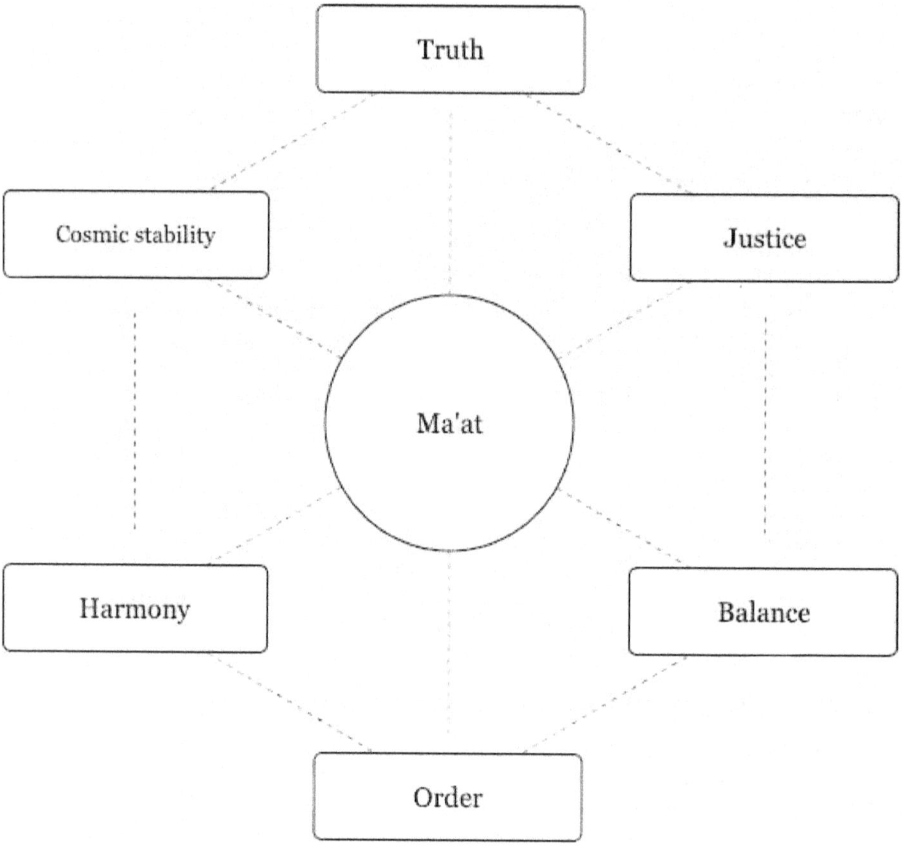

The pharaoh occupied a unique position in this system, one quite different from a Mesopotamian king. The pharaoh wasn't merely a ruler chosen by the gods to enforce justice. He was himself divine, a living god, and his central duty was to uphold Ma'at on earth. Because the pharaoh was the divine guarantor of cosmic order, his word carried the force of law directly. Egyptian law, in large part, was royal decree: the commands, judgments, and pronouncements of a god-king whose role was to embody and maintain Ma'at. There was less need for a written code when the source of justice was a living deity whose every ruling was, by definition, an expression of divine order.

This helps explain why Egypt developed no equivalent to Hammurabi's stone pillar. In Mesopotamia, kings were mortals who needed to demonstrate and justify their authority, and a published code served that purpose while also constraining and guiding officials. In Egypt, the pharaoh's divine status made such a monument less necessary. His authority came from his very nature as a god, not from a code he could point to. Justice flowed from him and from the principle of Ma'at he embodied, and it was administered through officials acting in his name rather than through a fixed body of written statutes that anyone could consult.

Yet Egypt was hardly a lawless place governed by nothing but royal whim. It had courts, judges, legal officials, and detailed procedures for resolving disputes. The vizier, the pharaoh's chief minister, oversaw the administration of justice and served as the highest judge below the king himself. Local courts, sometimes made up of respected community members, heard cases involving property, inheritance, contracts, and various wrongs. And though no comprehensive code survives, we have abundant records of actual legal cases, contracts, wills, and court proceedings that show Egyptian law operating in practice with considerable order and consistency.

These records reveal a legal culture that took procedure and evidence seriously. Egyptian courts heard testimony, considered documents, and sometimes administered oaths, with the parties swearing by the pharaoh or the gods to tell the truth. Written contracts were common and were treated as binding, covering sales, leases, loans, and marriage arrangements. Property could be bought, sold, and inherited according to established rules, and disputes over inheritance were frequent and carefully adjudicated.

So while Egypt lacked a codified body of law, it possessed a rich and functioning legal system, one grounded in the concept of Ma'at, administered under the authority of a divine king, and operating through courts and procedures that produced consistent and predictable outcomes.

The Egyptian case teaches us something important about the nature of law itself: that codification isn't the same thing as law, and that a society can have a developed, effective legal order without ever writing its rules into a comprehensive code. Egypt was governed by law for three thousand years. That law simply took a different form from the Mesopotamian model, rooted in a cosmic principle of order and expressed through the decrees of a god-king rather than through statutes carved in stone. When we study the history of law, we can't assume that written codes are the only, or even the primary, way law can exist. Egypt reminds us that law is fundamentally about maintaining order and justice in society, and that this can be achieved through many different means.

Women in Egypt enjoyed a legal standing that was remarkable for the ancient world and considerably better than in many neighboring societies. Egyptian women could own property in their own right, buy and sell goods, enter into contracts, bring lawsuits, serve as witnesses, and inherit and bequeath property. A married woman retained control over property she brought into the marriage and over property she acquired during it, and she could dispose of it as she wished. This relatively strong legal position for women reflects features of Egyptian society and its ideas about balance and order that gave women a more equal footing than they held in much of the ancient Near East, and it's one of the more striking aspects of Egyptian law when set against the patriarchal systems of its neighbors.

The Hittite Laws and early contract principles

North of Mesopotamia, in what's now Turkey, a people called the Hittites built a powerful empire in the second millennium BCE. At their height, around 1600 to 1180 BCE, the Hittites rivaled Egypt and Babylon as a great power of the ancient Near East, and they left behind their own collection of laws, preserved on clay tablets in their capital. The Hittite Laws offer a fascinating contrast to the Mesopotamian codes, because in important respects they took a notably different and, to modern eyes, more humane approach to punishment.

The Hittite Laws consist of around 200 provisions, and like the Mesopotamian codes they address a wide range of matters: personal injury, property, family, agriculture, commerce, and various offenses. But the philosophy behind their penalties diverges sharply from Hammurabi's. Where Hammurabi's code leaned heavily on physical retaliation, the eye for an eye, the Hittite Laws relied far more on compensation and restitution. For many offenses that would have brought bodily punishment or death under Babylonian law, Hittite law prescribed payment instead.

This difference is clearest in the treatment of injury and even homicide. Under Hittite law, a person who killed another might be required to pay compensation, sometimes in the form of handing over persons to the victim's family, rather than facing execution. If a man injured another and made him ill, he had to provide for the injured man's care and pay him for the time he couldn't work, along with a fee to the physician. This emphasis on compensating the victim and restoring the situation, rather than on inflicting matching harm on the offender, gives the Hittite Laws a different character from the retributive Mesopotamian model. The Hittites seemed more concerned with repairing the damage than with mirroring it.

We can even watch Hittite law becoming less harsh over time, which is one of the most interesting things about it. Some of the surviving Hittite legal texts explicitly note changes from earlier practice, recording that a penalty used to be one thing and is now another, usually milder. The texts sometimes state that formerly a certain offense was punished more severely, but now the punishment has been reduced. This is remarkable, because it gives us direct evidence of a legal system consciously reforming itself, deliberately moving away from harsher penalties toward gentler ones. We're not inferring this from comparing separate codes; the Hittites themselves recorded the change within their own laws. Few documents from the ancient world let us see legal reform happening this plainly, with the old rule and the new one set side by side.

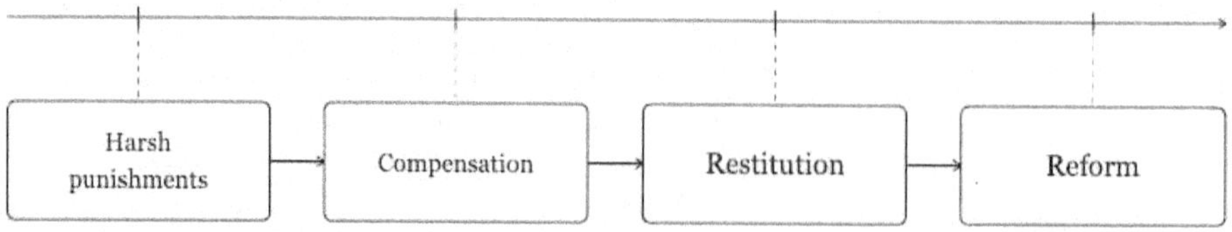

The Hittite Laws also reveal a society that took contracts and commercial arrangements seriously, and this is where they contribute something particularly valuable to the history of law. Many provisions deal with hiring, wages, prices, and the obligations arising from agreements between people. The laws set out fixed prices for a range of goods and standard wages for various kinds of labor, from harvesters to craftsmen. They addressed the responsibilities of people who hired animals or equipment, and the liability that followed if hired property was lost, damaged, or destroyed. If someone hired an ox and it died through the hirer's fault, the hirer had to make good the loss. These provisions rest on the principle that agreements create binding obligations, and that a person who takes on a responsibility through an agreement must answer for fulfilling it.

The concept underlying all of this is one that would grow into a central pillar of later legal systems: that a promise or agreement, freely entered into, creates a duty that the law will enforce. This is the germ of contract law, the body of rules governing the agreements people make with one another.

The Hittite Laws show this idea already at work in the second millennium BCE, with detailed provisions on what people owed each other under various arrangements and what happened when someone failed to meet an obligation. The society clearly relied on people keeping their agreements, and its law backed up those agreements with defined consequences for breaking them. Every modern contract, every deal enforced by a court today, descends from this ancient recognition that agreements bind and that the law stands behind them.

The Hittite Laws dealt extensively with agricultural life, as we'd expect from a society whose wealth rested on farming and herding. There were detailed provisions about land, crops, livestock, and the disputes that arose among neighbors sharing fields, water, and pasture. The laws addressed the theft of animals, the straying of livestock onto another's land, damage done by animals, and the responsibilities of shepherds and herders. Fire was a serious concern in a landscape of dry fields and stored grain, and the laws assigned liability for fires that spread and destroyed a neighbor's property. These provisions paint a picture of a rural society deeply concerned with protecting the agricultural resources on which everyone's survival depended.

The table below sets the three major Mesopotamian and Anatolian codes side by side, showing how differently they approached the punishment of serious wrongs.

Code	**Approximate Date**	**Primary Approach to Injury**	**Notable Feature**
Ur-Nammu	c. 2100 BCE	Monetary compensation	Earliest known written code
Hammurabi	c. 1750 BCE	Physical retaliation (talion), varied by class	Detailed class-based penalties
Hittite Laws	c. 1650–1500 BCE	Compensation and restitution	Recorded reduction of penalties over time

Taken together, these codes from Ur-Nammu, Hammurabi, and the Hittites demonstrate that even within the ancient Near East, a relatively compact region over a span of a few centuries, societies developed markedly different philosophies of law and punishment. Some leaned toward compensation, others toward retaliation. Some grew milder over time, others maintained severe penalties. Some built elaborate class distinctions into their penalties, others were more uniform. This variety is important, because it shows there was no single ancient approach to law, no uniform "primitive" system that all early societies shared. Instead there were many approaches, each reflecting the particular values, structures, and circumstances of the society that produced it. Law, even at this early stage, was shaped by culture, and different cultures reached different answers to the same basic questions.

The Mosaic Law and its civil applications

Among the legal traditions of the ancient Near East, one has exerted an influence far out of proportion to the size and power of the people who produced it. The laws attributed to Moses, preserved in the Hebrew Bible, came from a small nation that never rivaled Egypt, Babylon, or the Hittites in wealth or military might. Yet Mosaic Law shaped the legal and moral thinking of Western civilization more profoundly than any other ancient code, because it became foundational to Judaism, Christianity, and Islam, and through those religions it reached across continents and centuries in a way the great empire codes never did.

Mosaic Law is found primarily in the first five books of the Hebrew Bible, the Torah, and especially in the books of Exodus, Leviticus, Numbers, and Deuteronomy. It presents itself not as the work of a king but as law given by God to Moses, and through Moses to the entire people of Israel. This is a crucial difference from the Mesopotamian codes. Hammurabi's laws came from a king who claimed divine authorization, but the laws themselves were the king's, framed as his acts of justice. Mosaic Law, by contrast, is framed as coming directly from God, not merely authorized by God but authored by God. The law was understood as an expression of the divine will and as the terms of a covenant, a binding agreement between God and the people of Israel.

This covenant framework gave Mosaic Law a distinctive character. The law wasn't simply a set of rules imposed by authority; it was one side of a sacred relationship. God had chosen this people and delivered them, and in return they were bound to live according to His law. Keeping the law was an act of faithfulness to the covenant, and breaking it was a betrayal of the relationship with God, not merely a violation of a rule. This wove law, religion, and national identity together into a single fabric, so that to be part of the people was to live under the law, and to live under the law was to honor the bond with God.

The most famous portion of Mosaic Law is the Ten Commandments, the set of fundamental principles said to have been given to Moses on Mount Sinai. These commandments blend religious and moral duties in a way that captures the character of the whole tradition. Some concern the relationship between people and God: worship no other gods, make no idols, don't misuse God's name, keep the Sabbath holy. Others concern relationships among people: honor your parents, don't murder, don't commit adultery, don't steal, don't bear false witness, don't covet what belongs to others. This joining of religious obligation and social ethics reflects the Mosaic understanding that all of life, both the sacred and the everyday, fell under a single divine law.

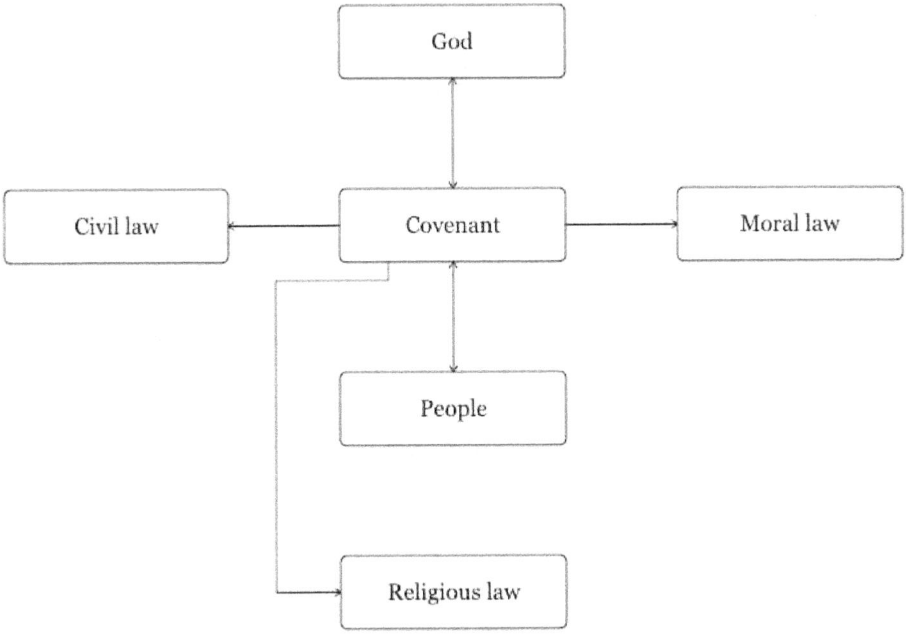

Beyond these broad principles, Mosaic Law contained extensive and detailed civil provisions, and this is the part most relevant to our subject, because it's here that the law functioned much like the other legal codes of the ancient Near East. The Torah lays out specific rules governing property, personal injury, theft, debt, contracts, marriage, inheritance, and the treatment of servants and the poor. In many places these provisions closely resemble the Mesopotamian codes, addressing the same practical problems in similar ways, which tells us that Mosaic Law didn't arise in isolation but shared in the broader legal culture of its region and drew on common ancient Near Eastern traditions.

The principle of proportionate justice appears in Mosaic Law in the familiar form of the talion. The Torah states that a person should give life for life, eye for eye, tooth for tooth, hand for hand, foot for foot. This is the same lex talionis found in Hammurabi's code, and it served the same function of limiting retaliation to a level matching the offense. Whether this was applied literally as physical retaliation or understood as a standard for calculating monetary compensation became a matter of interpretation, and in later Jewish legal tradition the rabbis generally understood it to mean monetary compensation rather than actual bodily retaliation. But the underlying principle, that the punishment should fit the crime and not exceed it, is the ancient idea of proportionate justice we've seen throughout this chapter.

Where Mosaic Law stands out is in its strong and repeated concern for the vulnerable members of society, a theme it develops with an insistence not matched in the other codes. Again and again the law commands the protection of the poor, the widow, the orphan, and the foreigner. It requires that farmers leave the edges of their fields unharvested and the gleanings ungathered, so the poor and the stranger could gather food. It forbids charging interest on loans to the poor and requires that a poor person's essential possessions taken as collateral be returned. It commands fair treatment of hired laborers, requiring that their wages be paid promptly and not held overnight. This emphasis on caring for the weak and the marginalized, framed as a religious duty owed to God, is one of the most distinctive features of Mosaic Law and one of its most lasting contributions to later Western ideas about justice and social obligation.

Mosaic Law also included provisions that were genuinely radical for their time, aimed at preventing permanent poverty and the concentration of wealth. The law established the Sabbatical year, in which every seventh year the land was to rest and debts owed by fellow Israelites were to be forgiven. Even more striking was the Jubilee year, occurring every fifty years, in which land that had been sold was to return to its original family owners and Israelites who'd fallen into bondage were to be freed. The idea behind these provisions was to prevent families from being permanently dispossessed of their land and permanently trapped in debt or servitude, periodically resetting economic relationships to preserve a rough balance and prevent the emergence of a permanent underclass. Whether the Jubilee was ever fully practiced remains uncertain, but as a legal principle it expresses a concern with long-term economic justice that was extraordinary in the ancient world.

The administration of Mosaic Law relied on judges and elders who heard disputes and rendered decisions, and the law set out standards for how justice was to be administered. Judges were commanded to judge fairly, to show no partiality, to take no bribes, and to give the same justice to the poor as to the rich and to the foreigner as to the native-born. The law required multiple witnesses to establish guilt in serious matters, forbidding conviction on the testimony of a single witness, a procedural protection against false accusation that reflects a concern with fair process. These standards of impartial judgment, equal treatment, and reliable evidence became part of the enduring legacy of Mosaic Law, feeding into later Western ideas about what a just legal process should look like.

The influence of Mosaic Law extends far beyond the ancient Israelites, and this is why it occupies such an important place in the history of law despite coming from a small nation. Through Judaism, it remained the foundation of Jewish life and law for thousands of years and continues to shape Jewish practice today. Through Christianity, it entered the moral and legal traditions of Europe and, eventually, much of the world, as Christian thinkers drew on the Hebrew Bible in developing their own ideas about law, morality, and justice. Through Islam, which also honors Moses as a prophet and shares many of these traditions, its influence reached further still. The moral principles of Mosaic Law, its concern for justice, its protection of the vulnerable, its insistence on fair judgment, became woven into the ethical foundations of Western civilization, giving this ancient code a reach and a longevity that the mightier empires of its age never achieved.

Discussion question: The ancient codes we've examined all claimed divine authority, whether through a god-king, a cosmic principle of order, or laws given directly by God. Why might early societies have needed to root their laws in the divine rather than simply presenting them as human decisions, and what does a legal system gain, and what might it lose, when it claims that its rules come from a source beyond human judgment?

Chapter 3: Law in Ancient Greece

The ancient codes of Mesopotamia and the Near East gave the world written law, fixed penalties, and the idea that rules should be public and knowable. But they shared one deep assumption: that law came from above, handed down by a god-king or a divine command, to be obeyed by everyone below.

The Greeks broke with this assumption in a way that changed history. In the city-states of Greece, and above all in Athens, people began to treat law not as something received from the gods but as something citizens made for themselves, debated among themselves, and could change when they saw fit. This was a revolution in how humans thought about law, and its consequences are still unfolding today.

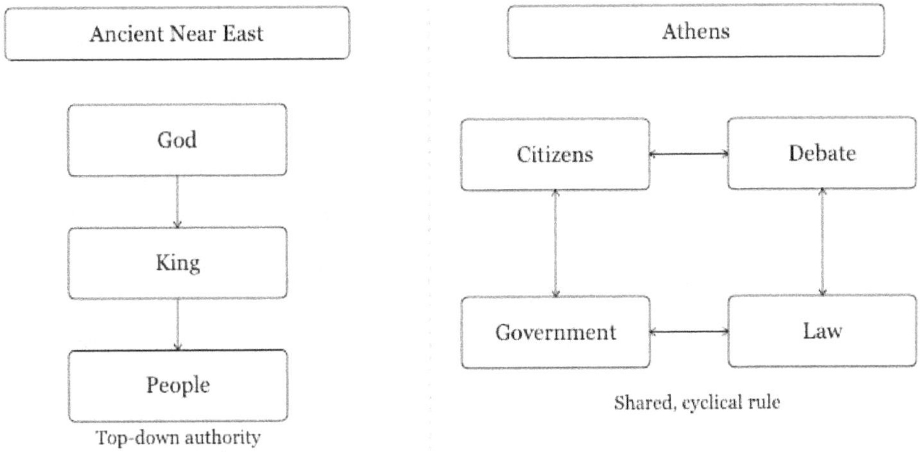

Greece in the first millennium BCE wasn't a unified country. It was a patchwork of independent city-states, each with its own government, its own customs, and its own laws. These city-states experimented with an astonishing variety of political arrangements: monarchies, oligarchies, tyrannies, and, most famously, democracy. Out of this restless political experimentation came new ideas about law, justice, and the relationship between citizens and the state, ideas that the Greeks not only put into practice but also examined, questioned, and argued about with a depth no previous civilization had attempted.

What makes Greek legal thought so important isn't just the specific laws the Greeks made, though some of those mattered enormously. It's that the Greeks were the first people we know of to ask, systematically and philosophically, what law actually is. What makes a law just? Where does law get its authority? Should we always obey the law, even when it's wrong? Is there a higher justice that human laws must answer to?

These questions, first posed clearly by Greek lawgivers and philosophers, became the permanent questions of legal philosophy, and every serious thinker about law since has had to grapple with them.

The reforms of Draco and Solon in Athens

Athens in the seventh century BCE was a troubled city. Power lay in the hands of a small aristocracy of wealthy landowners, and the law was unwritten, known only to the noble families who administered it. This gave the aristocrats enormous power, because they alone knew what the law was and could interpret it however they pleased. For ordinary Athenians, this was a source of deep resentment. A person accused of a crime couldn't consult the law to know their rights, because the law lived only in the memories and judgments of the nobles who ran the courts. Justice was whatever the aristocracy said it was, and the poor had little protection against the powerful.

The first major step toward changing this came around 621 BCE, when a lawgiver named Draco was appointed to write down the laws of Athens. This was itself a significant reform, because putting the laws in writing meant taking them out of the exclusive control of the aristocracy and making them public. Once the laws were written and posted, any Athenian could know what they were. The written law became a fixed reference that limited the arbitrary power of the noble judges, the same benefit that written codes had brought to earlier societies.

But Draco's laws became famous, or rather infamous, for one particular quality: their extraordinary harshness. The penalties Draco prescribed were brutally severe, and death was the punishment for a vast range of offenses, including quite minor ones. Stealing a cabbage or some fruit could bring the death penalty, just as murder did. When someone later asked why he'd made death the penalty for almost everything, the answer, according to ancient tradition, was that small crimes deserved death and he could find no greater punishment for the large ones. The laws were so bloody that they gave us a word we still use: draconian, meaning excessively harsh or severe. Draco's name became permanently attached to the idea of punishment out of all proportion to the offense.

Draco's harsh code didn't solve Athens's problems; it deepened them. The severity of the laws fell hardest on the poor, and the underlying grievances that troubled the city, the concentration of land and power among the wealthy, the crushing debt that burdened ordinary farmers, the deep divide between rich and poor, went unaddressed. By the early sixth century BCE, Athens was sliding toward civil war. Many poor farmers had fallen into debt so severe that they'd been forced to sell themselves or their children into slavery to pay what they owed, because under the existing law a person's own body could serve as security for a debt. The gap between the wealthy few and the impoverished many had grown so wide, and the resulting tensions so dangerous, that the city stood on the edge of violent upheaval.

Into this crisis stepped one of the most important figures in the history of law: Solon. Around 594 BCE, with Athens in turmoil, Solon was given extraordinary powers to reform the city's laws and constitution and to find a way out of the crisis. He was a man trusted by both sides, respected by the aristocracy but sympathetic to the plight of the poor, and he used his authority to enact reforms so significant that he's remembered as one of the founding figures of Athenian democracy and, indeed, of Western law itself.

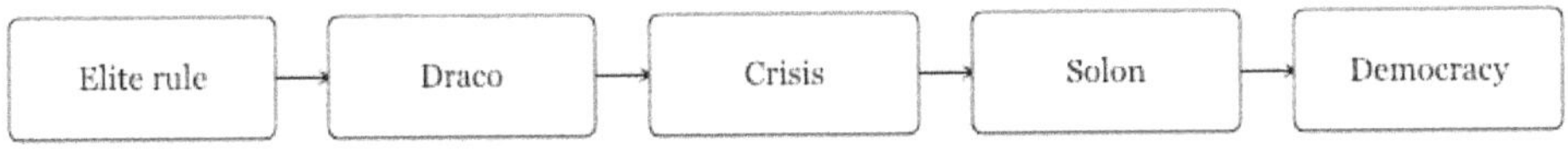

Solon's most dramatic and immediate reform addressed the debt crisis directly. He canceled outstanding debts and freed those who'd been enslaved for debt, a measure known as the seisachtheia, which means the "shaking off of burdens." He restored to freedom the Athenians who'd been sold into slavery over debt, even bringing back some who'd been sold abroad. And, crucially, he abolished the practice of debt bondage altogether, making it illegal to take a person's own body as security for a loan. From that point on, an Athenian could no longer be enslaved for failing to pay a debt. This single reform lifted an enormous weight from the poor and struck at one of the central injustices that had brought the city to the brink.

Solon then repealed nearly all of Draco's brutal laws, keeping only the provisions concerning homicide. In place of Draco's blanket use of the death penalty, Solon established a system of penalties that fit the seriousness of the offense, a far more measured and proportionate approach to punishment. This move away from indiscriminate severity toward penalties matched to the gravity of the crime was a major advance, and it reflected Solon's broader concern with fairness and balance in the law.

Solon's reforms went well beyond debt and punishment to reshape the whole structure of Athenian society and government. He reorganized the citizen body into classes based on wealth rather than birth, so that a person's political rights and duties depended on their property rather than on the family they were born into. This mattered because it broke the aristocracy's monopoly on power, opening a path by which a person of common birth who acquired wealth could gain political standing. Solon also opened participation in the courts and assembly more widely, allowing ordinary citizens a role in the governance of the city that they'd previously been denied.

One of Solon's most consequential innovations was to allow any citizen, not just the injured party, to bring a legal case on behalf of someone who'd been wronged. Previously, only the victim or the victim's family could initiate a prosecution, which meant that the weak, who had no powerful family to act for them, often had no recourse at all when they were wronged. By allowing any citizen to prosecute on another's behalf, Solon gave the community as a whole a stake in upholding justice and offered protection to those who couldn't protect themselves. This was a step toward the idea that a wrong against one member of the community was a matter of concern for the whole community, an idea that lies near the heart of what we now think of as public justice and criminal law.

Solon was careful not to hand ultimate power to any single person or faction. After completing his reforms, tradition holds that he left Athens for ten years, making the Athenians swear to keep his laws unchanged until he returned, so that no one could pressure him into altering them and the reforms would have time to take root. Whether or not every detail of this story is accurate, it captures something essential about Solon's aim: he sought not to make himself a ruler but to establish a framework of law under which the city could govern itself. He famously described his role as standing between the contending parties, holding a strong shield over both and letting neither side win an unjust victory over the other, refusing to become a tyrant even when he had the chance.

The table below contrasts the two lawgivers whose work set Athens on the path toward democratic law.

	Draco (c. 621 BCE)	**Solon (c. 594 BCE)**
Main achievement	First written laws of Athens	Sweeping legal and constitutional reform
Approach to penalties	Death for nearly all offenses	Penalties proportioned to the offense
Treatment of debt	Left debt bondage intact	Abolished debt bondage, canceled debts
Effect on the poor	Deepened their hardship	Freed the enslaved, protected the weak
Lasting reputation	Gave us the word "draconian"	Founding figure of Athenian democracy

Solon didn't create democracy outright, and Athens would go through further upheavals, including a period of tyranny, before its democracy reached its mature form later in the sixth and fifth centuries BCE. But Solon laid the essential groundwork. By abolishing debt slavery, moderating the harshness of the law, opening political participation beyond the aristocracy, and giving ordinary citizens a role in justice, he established the principles on which Athenian democracy would be built. His reforms embodied a new idea that would prove world-changing: that law could be an instrument of justice for the whole community, deliberately crafted to balance competing interests and protect the weak from the strong, rather than a weapon wielded by the powerful to preserve their own dominance.

The Athenian jury system and public trials

By the fifth and fourth centuries BCE, Athenian democracy had matured into a system that placed the administration of justice directly in the hands of ordinary citizens. This was one of the most remarkable features of Athenian law and one of the sharpest breaks from everything that had come before. In the ancient Near East, justice had been administered by kings, appointed officials, priests, and professional judges, people set apart by their office or their expertise. In democratic Athens, justice was administered by the citizens themselves, drawn from the general population, deciding cases as a body. There were no professional judges directing the proceedings and no lawyers arguing the cases. Ordinary Athenians ran the courts.

At the center of this system stood the popular courts, and the juries that decided cases in them were enormous by any standard. An Athenian jury might number several hundred citizens, and in some important cases the number ran into the thousands. A typical jury for an ordinary case might consist of 201 or 501 jurors, and the size could go far higher. These weren't the small juries of a dozen people that we're used to. They were massive assemblies of citizens, and their sheer size served an important purpose: it made bribery and intimidation practically impossible. You simply can't bribe or threaten hundreds or thousands of people, so the very scale of the Athenian jury protected the integrity of its verdicts.

Jurors were chosen by lot from among the citizen body, and this method of selection reflected a principle deep in Athenian democratic thought. **Selection by lot, rather than by election or appointment, meant that any citizen might be called to serve, and that the responsibility of judging fell on the ordinary members of the community rather than on a special class of officials**. Each year, a large pool of citizens put themselves forward as potential jurors, and from this pool, jurors for particular cases were selected randomly on the day of the trial through an elaborate allotment procedure designed to prevent tampering. The Athenians developed an ingenious device, a stone slab with slots called a kleroterion, to randomize the selection of jurors and ensure that no one could predict or manipulate which citizens would hear a given case.

The trials themselves worked very differently from what we're used to today, and understanding those differences reveals a great deal about Athenian ideas of justice. There were no lawyers. Each party had to present their own case, speaking on their own behalf before the jury. A person who wasn't a skilled speaker was at a real disadvantage, and a market developed for the services of professional speechwriters, called logographers, who would compose a speech for a litigant to memorize and deliver as if it were his own. Some of the finest surviving examples of ancient Greek prose are the courtroom speeches written by these logographers, which give us a vivid window into the disputes, the personalities, and the legal reasoning of the Athenian courts.

Trials moved quickly, because they were strictly timed. Each side was allotted a set amount of time to make its case, measured by a water clock called a klepsydra, which let water flow from one vessel to another and marked the passage of time by the emptying of the container. When your water ran out, your time was up, whether you'd finished or not. This kept trials short, and most were completed in a single day. There was no drawn-out process of the kind familiar in modern courts, no lengthy accumulation of evidence and argument over weeks or months. Both sides spoke, the water clock measured out their time, and the matter was decided that same day.

After both sides had spoken and presented their evidence and witnesses, the jury voted immediately, without any period of deliberation and without discussing the case among themselves. There was no jury room where jurors debated toward a verdict, no requirement of unanimity, no judge instructing them on the law. Each juror simply cast a secret ballot, and the verdict was decided by a simple majority. If more jurors voted to convict than to acquit, the defendant was convicted; if not, acquitted. The Athenians used bronze ballot disks with a hollow or solid hub to indicate a vote for one side or the other, and the secret ballot protected jurors from any pressure over how they'd voted.

This system had real strengths and real weaknesses, and it's worth being honest about both. On the positive side, it embodied the democratic ideal in a direct and powerful way, putting justice genuinely in the hands of the people and making the courts a true expression of the citizen body rather than an instrument of any elite. The large juries and secret ballots made corruption extremely difficult, and the participation of ordinary citizens gave the courts a broad legitimacy. The system reflected a profound trust in the collective judgment of ordinary people, a trust that lay at the very heart of Athenian democracy.

On the negative side, the system had no safeguards that we'd now consider essential. Without judges to guide them on the law, without lawyers to test the evidence, and without any deliberation before voting, juries could be swayed by emotion, by clever rhetoric, by prejudice, or by the personal appeal of a litigant rather than by the actual merits of the case. Juries decided on the basis of persuasive speeches, and a skilled speaker or a well-written speech could win a case that perhaps didn't deserve to be won. There was no appeal from a jury's verdict, so a wrong decision stood without any means of correction.

The most famous, and most troubling, illustration of these dangers is the trial of Socrates in 399 BCE. The philosopher Socrates was brought before an Athenian jury, charged with impiety and with corrupting the youth of the city. A jury of hundreds of citizens heard the case, and by a majority they found him guilty and condemned him to death. Socrates was made to drink poison hemlock, and one of the greatest thinkers in history was executed by the democratic courts of Athens on charges that many, then and since, have regarded as unjust. His trial and death stand as a permanent reminder that democratic justice, for all its virtues, can go terribly wrong, and that the collective judgment of the majority is no guarantee against injustice. The very system that gave Athens its remarkable popular courts also put Socrates to death.

Plato and Aristotle on justice and governance

The trial and execution of Socrates cast a long shadow over Greek thought, and nowhere longer than over his greatest student, Plato. Watching the democratic courts of Athens condemn his teacher to death on charges he considered unjust shaped Plato's lifelong suspicion of democracy and his search for a better foundation for law and government. Out of that search came some of the most influential writing about justice, law, and the state ever produced, work that has occupied philosophers for nearly two and a half thousand years and continues to do so.

Plato, who lived from around 428 to 348 BCE, explored questions of justice most fully in his great work the Republic. The central question of the Republic is deceptively simple: what is justice? Plato wasn't satisfied with the ordinary answers, that justice means following the law, or giving people what they're owed, or helping friends and harming enemies. He wanted to know what justice really is, at the deepest level, both in the individual soul and in the state. His answer was that justice is a kind of harmony, a proper ordering in which each part performs its own proper function and doesn't interfere with the others.

In Plato's vision of the just state, society is divided into classes, each suited to a particular role: the producers who supply the material needs of the city, the guardians or warriors who defend it, and the rulers who govern it. Justice, for Plato, consists in each class doing the work it's naturally suited for and not meddling in the work of the others. The producers should produce, the warriors should protect, and the rulers should rule, each staying in their proper place. When every part of society performs its proper function in harmony with the others, the state is just, just as a person is just when reason, spirit, and appetite are properly ordered within the soul.

Plato's most famous and controversial idea was that the rulers of the just state should be philosophers. He argued that political power should be held by those who possess genuine knowledge of what is good and just, the philosopher-kings, rather than by ordinary people swayed by opinion, emotion, and self-interest. Only those who've dedicated their lives to the pursuit of wisdom and who truly understand justice, Plato held, are fit to rule. His disillusionment with Athenian democracy runs right through this idea. He'd seen the democratic courts kill Socrates, and he'd concluded that ordinary people, however numerous, lacked the knowledge to govern well and were too easily led astray. Better, he thought, to entrust rule to the wise few who actually knew what justice required.

(Jacques Louis David - The Death of Socrates)

This is a deeply anti-democratic vision, and it's important to recognize it as such. Plato didn't trust the judgment of ordinary citizens, and he didn't believe that justice could be safely left to majority vote. He wanted rule by knowledge, not rule by numbers.

Critics from his own time to the present have pointed out the obvious dangers in this: who decides who the truly wise are, and what prevents rule by the supposedly wise from becoming simply another form of tyranny, dressed up as philosophy? But even those who reject Plato's conclusions have found his questions inescapable. Is expertise relevant to governing? Should everyone's opinion count equally on every question? Can ordinary people be trusted to govern themselves wisely? These questions, which Plato pressed with unmatched force, remain alive in every debate about democracy today.

In his later work, the Laws, Plato took a somewhat different and more practical approach. Having recognized that the ideal state ruled by philosopher-kings might be impossible to achieve in the real world, he turned to the question of how to design the best possible system of laws for an actual city. In the Laws, written law itself takes center stage as the foundation of a well-ordered society, standing in for the perfect wisdom of the philosopher-king that no real ruler could possess. Plato came to see carefully crafted law, applied consistently, as the next best thing to the rule of the truly wise, a way of embedding reason and justice in permanent rules that could govern a city even in the absence of perfect rulers. This shift, from the rule of wise persons to the rule of wise laws, is significant, and it points toward the idea that would prove so central to later legal thought: that it's better to be governed by law than by the will of any individual, however wise.

Plato's student **Aristotle**, who lived from 384 to 322 BCE, developed these ideas in directions that would prove even more influential for the history of law, and his approach differed from his teacher's in important ways. Where Plato reached for the ideal, seeking the perfect form of justice and the perfect state, Aristotle was more practical, more empirical, and more attentive to how things actually work in the messy real world. He studied the constitutions of many actual Greek city-states, gathering and comparing them, and he built his conclusions from observation of real political life rather than from abstract ideals alone. This grounded, comparative method gave his thinking about law a durability that has kept it relevant across the centuries.

Aristotle made a distinction that has shaped legal thinking ever since: the distinction between different kinds of justice. He recognized that justice isn't a single thing but takes different forms in different situations. Distributive justice concerns the fair distribution of goods, honors, and resources among the members of a community, the question of who should get what. Corrective justice, which Aristotle also called rectificatory justice, concerns the righting of wrongs, the restoration of a fair balance when one person has wronged another, whether by breaking an agreement or causing an injury. This distinction, between the just distribution of benefits and burdens on the one hand and the just correction of wrongs on the other, became fundamental to legal philosophy and remains a basic tool for thinking about what justice requires in different circumstances.

Aristotle also gave deep thought to the relationship between written law and fairness in particular cases, and here he introduced a concept of lasting importance: equity. He recognized that written laws, because they're general rules stated in advance, can't anticipate every situation that might arise, and that applying a general rule rigidly to a particular case can sometimes produce an unjust result the lawmaker never intended. When this happens, Aristotle argued, justice requires that we correct the law, judging the particular case as the lawmaker would have judged it had he foreseen the situation. This is equity: the correction of law where it falls short because of its generality. Aristotle's insight that strict application of general rules must sometimes yield to the demands of fairness in the individual case became a permanent feature of legal thought and, much later, would give rise to entire systems of equitable justice designed to soften the rigidity of the ordinary law.

Perhaps Aristotle's most important contribution to legal and political thought was his powerful argument for the rule of law over the rule of individuals, and this idea sits at the very foundation of how we think about law and government today. Aristotle asked whether it's better to be governed by the best individual or by the best laws, and he came down firmly on the side of law. An individual ruler, however excellent, is subject to passion, emotion, appetite, and self-interest, forces that can cloud judgment and corrupt decisions. Law, by contrast, is reason free from passion, a standard that doesn't get angry, doesn't grow greedy, and doesn't play favorites. To be ruled by law rather than by the will of any person is to be ruled by reason rather than by desire. This argument, that law should be sovereign and that even rulers should be subject to it, became one of the cornerstones of Western political and legal thought and remains central to how we understand constitutional government and the rule of law today.

Natural law theory in Greek philosophy

Among all the ideas the Greeks contributed to legal thought, one has proven especially powerful and especially durable: the idea of natural law. This is the notion that there exists a higher law, grounded in nature or reason, that stands above the laws made by particular societies, and against which those human-made laws can be measured and judged. It's an idea with enormous consequences, because it means that the law of a given city or state isn't the final word on justice. There's a higher standard, and a human law that violates it can be criticized as unjust, and perhaps even denied the status of true law altogether.

To understand why this idea was so significant, we need to grasp a distinction the Greeks drew between two kinds of things. On one side was what the Greeks called nomos, meaning law, custom, or convention, the rules that particular human societies make and that vary from place to place. On the other side was physis, meaning nature, the way things really are independent of human choice or agreement.

Human laws are nomos: they differ from one city to another, they change over time, and they're the product of human decision. But is there anything about justice that belongs to physis, that's true by nature rather than merely by human convention, and that holds everywhere regardless of what any particular society happens to decree? This question, of whether justice is merely conventional or has a foundation in nature, became one of the great debates of Greek philosophy.

The idea that there's a higher, natural justice above human law found powerful early expression in Greek literature, most famously in Sophocles' tragedy Antigone. In the play, King Creon has issued a decree forbidding the burial of Antigone's brother, who died fighting against the city, and declaring that his body must be left unburied as a punishment. Antigone defies the decree and buries her brother anyway, and when Creon confronts her, she justifies her defiance by appealing to a higher law. She tells him that his decree, being the command of a mortal man, couldn't override the unwritten and unchanging laws of the gods, which have existed forever and which no human proclamation can set aside. Antigone's appeal to an eternal, unwritten law that stands above the decrees of rulers is one of the most powerful early statements of the natural law idea, dramatizing the conflict between human law and a higher justice that human law must answer to.

The philosophers gave this intuition a more systematic form. Various Greek thinkers explored the idea that reason, which all human beings share, could discover principles of justice valid everywhere and always, not just in one city or another. If justice has a foundation in nature and in reason rather than in mere custom, then it isn't simply whatever a particular society decides it is. It's something that can be discovered through the exercise of reason and that holds universally, binding all people regardless of the particular laws of their particular states. This was a profound idea, because it suggested that beneath the endless variety of human laws and customs there might lie a common, natural standard of justice accessible to human reason.

This line of thought reached its fullest ancient development somewhat later, in the philosophy of the Stoics, a school that arose in the Greek world and profoundly influenced Roman thought. The Stoics developed the idea of natural law more fully than anyone before them, teaching that the universe is governed by reason, a rational principle they called the logos, and that this same reason is present in every human being. Because all people share in this universal reason, the Stoics held, there's a natural law, grounded in reason itself, that applies to all human beings everywhere, transcending the boundaries of individual states and the differences among their particular laws. All people, by virtue of their shared rational nature, are subject to this single natural law and belong, in a sense, to a single universal community governed by it.

The Stoic conception of natural law carried implications that were genuinely radical for the ancient world. If all human beings share in reason and are subject to the same natural law, then in some fundamental sense all human beings are equal, bound together by their common rational nature regardless of whether they're Greek or barbarian, free or slave, citizen or foreigner. This idea of a universal human community united by a common law and a shared rational nature stood in striking contrast to the ordinary assumptions of the ancient world, which drew sharp distinctions between Greeks and non-Greeks, free persons and slaves, and citizens and outsiders. The Stoics planted a seed, the idea of a common humanity subject to a common natural law, that would grow across the centuries and eventually feed into modern ideas of universal human rights.

The natural law idea would go on to have an immense influence on the history of law, and it's worth seeing where it leads, because the thread runs directly from these Greek beginnings to the present. It passed from the Stoics into Roman legal thought, where jurists spoke of a law of nature underlying and informing the actual laws of Rome. It was taken up by Christian thinkers, who identified natural law with the law of God written into creation and accessible to human reason, weaving it deeply into medieval philosophy and theology. It provided the foundation for the theories of natural rights that emerged in the seventeenth and eighteenth centuries, the idea that human beings possess certain rights by nature that no government may rightly violate. And it stands behind the modern concept of universal human rights, the notion that there are standards of justice binding on all governments everywhere, against which even the laws of sovereign states can be judged and found wanting.

The table below summarizes the major Greek contributions to legal thought that we've traced in this chapter, ideas that between them laid much of the intellectual foundation for how the Western world would come to understand law.

Contribution	Key Figure(s)	Core Idea
Written, public law	Draco, Solon	Law should be knowable to all, not the secret of an elite
Proportionate justice	Solon	Penalties should fit the seriousness of the offense
Popular justice	Athenian democracy	Ordinary citizens should administer the law
Types of justice	Aristotle	Distributive and corrective justice are distinct
Equity	Aristotle	Fairness must correct rigid rules in particular cases
Rule of law	Aristotle	Law, as reason without passion, should govern, not individuals
Natural law	Sophocles, the Stoics	A higher law grounded in nature stands above human law

What the Greeks gave the history of law, in the end, wasn't primarily a body of specific statutes. It was a way of thinking about law: the conviction that law is a human creation open to reason and debate, the practice of examining law critically and asking what justice truly requires, and the enduring idea that there's a higher standard against which all human laws can be measured. The Greeks were the first to make law an object of serious philosophical reflection, and the questions they raised, about the nature of justice, the authority of law, the proper form of government, and the existence of a natural law above human law, became the permanent questions that all later legal thought would have to confront. In this sense, the Greeks are the true founders of legal philosophy, and their influence runs through every serious attempt to understand law that has come after them.

Discussion question: Athens trusted ordinary citizens to administer justice directly, yet those same citizens condemned Socrates to death, while Plato distrusted the people and wanted the wisest to rule, yet couldn't say who should decide who the wisest are. Given that both popular judgment and rule by experts can fail badly, is there any way to design a legal system that guards against the weaknesses of both, or must every system finally place its trust somewhere and accept the risk that comes with it?

Chapter 4: Roman Law and Its Lasting Structure

If you sign a contract today, rent an apartment, form a company, or take a dispute to court, you're using tools that Roman lawyers built. No other legal tradition in history has reached so far or lasted so long. The Greeks gave the world philosophy about law, deep questions about justice and the nature of legal authority. But it was the Romans who built law into a working system, a vast, detailed, practical machinery for handling every kind of human dispute and transaction. And that machinery proved so well-made that it outlived the empire that created it by more than a thousand years and still shapes the legal systems of most of the world today.

Rome grew from a small city on the banks of the Tiber into the master of the entire Mediterranean world, ruling for centuries over an empire that stretched from Britain to the Middle East, from the Rhine to the Sahara. Governing such an empire, with its enormous population and its endless commerce and conflict, demanded a legal system of unprecedented sophistication. The Romans rose to this challenge and produced the most influential body of law the world has ever known. Their genius wasn't for grand theory. It was for the practical work of law: for defining rights and obligations precisely, for developing clear rules to handle real problems, and for building a coherent legal system out of centuries of accumulated experience.

What the Romans created wasn't just a set of laws for their own time and place. It was a legal science, a systematic and rational approach to law, worked out by generations of skilled legal thinkers. This Roman legal science was eventually gathered and preserved in a great compilation that transmitted it to later ages, and through that compilation Roman law became the foundation of the civil law tradition that governs continental Europe, Latin America, and much of the rest of the world to this day. To understand modern law, you have to understand Rome, because so much of what we take for granted in law was first worked out by Roman minds.

The Twelve Tables and early Roman codification

The story of Roman law begins, much like the story of Athenian law, with a conflict between the powerful and the ordinary. In the early Roman Republic, around the middle of the fifth century BCE, Roman society was divided between two orders: the patricians, the aristocratic families who held power and privilege, and the plebeians, the ordinary citizens who made up the bulk of the population. The law was unwritten, and it was administered and interpreted exclusively by the patricians, who alone knew its content. This gave the aristocracy a source of power much like the one the Athenian nobles had enjoyed, and it gave the plebeians a grievance much like the one the Athenian poor had felt.

The plebeians resented deeply that the law was hidden from them, known only to the patrician priests and magistrates who could interpret it however they wished. A plebeian brought before a court had no way to know the law he was being judged by, and no protection against a patrician judge who might simply declare the law to be whatever suited him. The demand for the law to be written down and made public became a central plebeian cause in the long struggle between the two orders known as the Conflict of the Orders, and around 450 BCE, after sustained pressure, the plebeians finally won it.

The result was the Twelve Tables, the first written code of Roman law and the foundation on which all later Roman law was built. According to tradition, a commission of ten men, the decemviri, was appointed to draft the laws, and the finished code was inscribed on twelve tablets, said to have been made of bronze, and displayed publicly in the Roman Forum for all to see. For the first time, the law of Rome was written, public, and accessible, taking it out of the exclusive control of the patrician class and giving ordinary Romans the ability to know the rules they lived under.

The Twelve Tables became something close to sacred in Roman culture, a reverence that tells us how important they were to the Roman sense of who they were. Roman schoolchildren for centuries were made to memorize the Twelve Tables as a basic part of their education, learning them by heart the way children in other times and places memorized scripture.

The Romans regarded them as the source and foundation of their entire law, and even as the law grew and developed enormously over the following thousand years, the Twelve Tables remained the honored root from which it all had grown. This deep respect for the Twelve Tables reflects the Roman reverence for law itself and for the tradition and continuity of their legal system, a reverence that became one of the defining features of Roman civilization.

The content of the Twelve Tables covered the practical concerns of an early agricultural and commercial society, addressing the matters that mattered most in daily Roman life. The tables dealt with legal procedure, setting out how a person was to be summoned to court and how cases were to proceed. They addressed debt, family relationships, inheritance, property, and various wrongs, laying down rules for the concerns that generated the most conflict among Romans. Some of the provisions strike us as harsh, in keeping with the severity of the age, including penalties that seem brutal by modern standards and rules that gave the male head of a household, the paterfamilias, extensive power over his wife, children, and slaves. But taken as a whole, the Twelve Tables represented a major step toward a rational, public, and orderly system of law, and they established the principle that the law should be knowable to all citizens.

Perhaps the most significant thing about the Twelve Tables wasn't any particular rule they contained but the principle they embodied: that Romans of all classes were subject to a common, publicly known law. This was a foundational idea for the Roman legal tradition and, indeed, for the Western legal tradition as a whole. It meant that law wasn't the private preserve of an elite but the shared possession of the whole community, a standard that applied to everyone and that everyone could know. From this foundation, over the following centuries, the Romans would build one of the most sophisticated legal systems in human history, but they always looked back to the Twelve Tables as the beginning, the moment when Roman law first became public, written, and common to all.

The development of the Roman legal profession

Roman law didn't stay frozen in the form the Twelve Tables gave it. Over the following centuries, it grew and developed into an immense and sophisticated body of law, and the engine of this development was a remarkable group of people: the Roman jurists. These were the legal experts who made Roman law what it became, and the emergence of this class of legal specialists is one of the most important developments in the entire history of law, because the Romans essentially invented the legal profession and the idea of law as a specialized field of expertise and study.

In the early Republic, legal knowledge had been controlled by the priests, who guarded the forms and procedures of the law as a kind of sacred mystery. But over time, legal expertise passed into the hands of secular specialists, learned men who devoted themselves to the study and interpretation of law. These were the jurists, and they occupied a distinctive and prestigious position in Roman society. They weren't lawyers in the modern sense of advocates who argued cases in court for a fee; that was a separate role, filled by orators skilled in persuasion. The jurists were something different and, in the long run, far more important: they were legal scholars and advisers, experts in the substance of the law itself who studied it, interpreted it, developed it, and gave authoritative opinions on it.

The jurists shaped Roman law primarily through the giving of opinions, and understanding how this worked reveals the genius of the Roman approach to legal development. When a legal question arose, whether from a private citizen facing a dispute, a magistrate needing guidance, or a judge deciding a case, people would turn to a jurist for his opinion on the point of law. The jurist would consider the question and give his response, his considered view of what the law required in the matter at hand. These opinions, given by the most respected jurists, carried great authority, and over time the accumulated opinions of the jurists became a major source of Roman law in their own right, developing and refining it case by case, question by question.

This method of legal development had a distinctive character that gave Roman law its particular strength. Roman law grew not primarily through legislation, the passing of statutes, but through this ongoing process of expert interpretation and opinion.

Faced with a new problem, the jurists would reason from established principles to work out the right answer, extending and refining the law to cover situations the old rules hadn't anticipated. This gave Roman law a remarkable capacity to develop and adapt while maintaining continuity with its foundations, growing organically to meet new needs without ever losing its coherence. The jurists brought to this work a rigorous, analytical cast of mind, defining concepts with precision, drawing careful distinctions, and building up a body of law that was systematic and rational to a degree no previous legal tradition had achieved.

The jurists also wrote, and their writings became fundamental to Roman law and to its transmission to later ages. They produced commentaries on the law, treatises on particular legal subjects, collections of legal opinions, and textbooks for teaching law to students. The greatest of the Roman jurists, men like Gaius, Papinian, Ulpian, and Paulus, who worked mainly in the second and third centuries CE during the classical period of Roman law, produced writings of such quality and authority that they became the core of the Roman legal tradition. Their works analyzed the law with extraordinary skill and clarity, and it's largely through their writings, preserved in later compilations, that the achievement of Roman legal science came down to us. Gaius in particular wrote an introductory textbook called the Institutes, a clear and systematic exposition of Roman law designed for students, which survived and became one of the most influential legal texts in history, shaping how law was taught and organized for centuries.

The prestige of the jurists in Roman society was considerable, and it reflected the high value the Romans placed on law and legal expertise. To be a jurist was to occupy a respected and honored position, and many of the leading jurists were men of high social standing who combined their legal work with distinguished public careers. Some emperors granted certain jurists the right to give opinions that carried special authority, effectively making their views binding, which shows how important the emperors considered the work of the jurists to the functioning of the legal system. The Romans understood that a sophisticated society needed a sophisticated legal system, and that such a system required specialists who devoted their lives to mastering and developing the law. In creating and honoring this class of legal experts, the Romans established the model of the legal profession that persists to this day, the idea that law is a specialized discipline requiring dedicated study and expertise.

Justinian's Corpus Juris Civilis

By the sixth century CE, the western half of the Roman Empire had fallen, overrun by Germanic peoples, and the great days of classical Roman law were long past. But in the eastern half of the empire, centered on Constantinople and known to later ages as the Byzantine Empire, Roman rule continued, and it was here that Roman law received its final and most consequential form. The emperor Justinian, who reigned from 527 to 565 CE, undertook a project that would preserve the achievement of Roman legal science and transmit it to the future, and this project stands as one of the most important events in the entire history of law.

By Justinian's time, Roman law had accumulated over a thousand years of development, and it existed in a vast, sprawling, and often contradictory mass of material. There were the ancient statutes, the edicts of the magistrates, the accumulated opinions and writings of generations of jurists, and the decrees of the emperors, all piled up over the centuries into an enormous body of law that had grown unwieldy and confusing. Much of it was contradictory, outdated, or simply too voluminous to manage, and finding the actual law on any given point had become a daunting task. Justinian resolved to bring order to this chaos, to gather the whole inheritance of Roman law, sort out its contradictions, and organize it into a clear, coherent, and authoritative form.

Justinian appointed a commission of legal experts, led by a brilliant official named Tribonian, to carry out this immense undertaking. The commission worked with remarkable speed and thoroughness, sifting through the massive accumulation of Roman legal materials, selecting what was valuable, discarding what was obsolete or contradictory, and organizing the result into a systematic whole. The product of their labors was a comprehensive compilation of Roman law that later ages would call the Corpus Juris Civilis, meaning the "Body of Civil Law," a name given to it centuries afterward. This compilation preserved the essence of Roman legal science and became the vehicle through which Roman law reached the modern world.

The Corpus Juris Civilis consisted of several distinct parts, each serving a different purpose, and together they formed a complete statement of Roman law. The first part was the Code, a collection of the imperial legislation, the laws issued by the emperors, gathered together and organized by subject, with obsolete and contradictory laws removed. The second and most important part for the history of legal science was the Digest, also called the Pandects, an enormous compilation of extracts from the writings of the classical jurists, organized by subject. The Digest preserved the accumulated wisdom of Roman legal science, the analysis and reasoning of the great jurists, condensing their vast writings into a systematic collection that became the heart of the whole compilation and the richest source of classical Roman law that survives.

The third part was the Institutes, a textbook for students, based largely on the earlier Institutes of Gaius, designed to introduce beginners to the principles of Roman law in a clear and orderly way. The Institutes gave students a systematic overview of the law before they tackled the more demanding Digest and Code, and it became the standard introduction to Roman law for centuries. A fourth part, the Novels, consisted of the new laws that Justinian issued after the rest of the compilation was

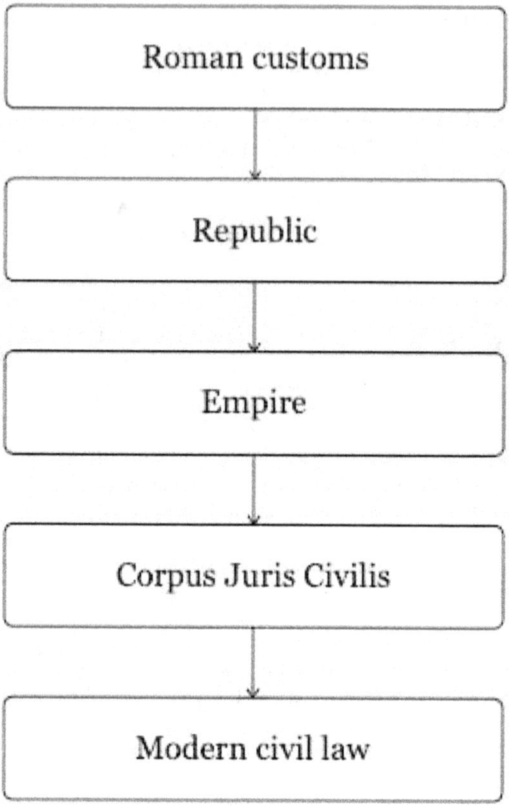

completed, added to keep the collection current. Together, these four parts, the Code, the Digest, the Institutes, and the Novels, made up the Corpus Juris Civilis, the great monument of Roman law.

The table below lays out the four parts of Justinian's compilation and what each one contained.

Part	Latin Name	Content	Purpose
The Code	Codex	Imperial legislation, organized by subject	To collect the emperors' laws in order
The Digest	Digesta (Pandectae)	Extracts from the classical jurists' writings	To preserve Roman legal science
The Institutes	Institutiones	Elementary textbook of legal principles	To teach law to students

The Novels	Novellae	New laws issued after the compilation	To keep the collection up to date

The importance of Justinian's compilation to the history of law can hardly be overstated, and its influence reaches directly into the present. In the short term, it provided the Byzantine Empire with a clear and authoritative statement of its law.

But its greatest significance lay far in the future. In the western half of the former empire, the Corpus Juris Civilis was largely forgotten during the early medieval centuries, as the sophisticated legal culture of Rome gave way to the simpler customs of the Germanic kingdoms. Then, around the end of the eleventh century, the Digest was rediscovered in the West, and its rediscovery set off a revival of Roman legal study that transformed European law.

Scholars at the newly emerging universities of medieval Europe, beginning at Bologna in Italy, took up the study of the rediscovered Corpus Juris Civilis with tremendous enthusiasm, and it became the foundation of legal education and legal science across the continent. Generation after generation of scholars studied, taught, and commented on Justinian's compilation, and through their work the principles and concepts of Roman law spread throughout continental Europe and shaped the development of its legal systems. This is why the legal systems of continental Europe, and of the many parts of the world that later adopted European law, are called civil law systems: they descend from the civil law of Rome as preserved in Justinian's Corpus Juris Civilis. Justinian's project, undertaken to preserve the law of a fading empire, ended up transmitting Roman legal science across the centuries and making it the foundation of the legal systems that govern much of the world today.

Roman concepts of property, contract, and tort

The lasting power of Roman law rests not only on the fact that it was preserved and transmitted but on the quality of the law itself, the sophistication and refinement of the legal concepts the Romans developed. In working out the rules for handling the endless variety of human disputes and transactions, the Roman jurists developed concepts of extraordinary precision and durability, concepts so well-designed that they remain the basic building blocks of law today. Three areas in particular show the depth of the Roman achievement: property, contract, and the law of wrongs, and these three areas between them form much of the foundation of private law across the world.

Property was one of the areas where Roman legal thought reached its greatest refinement, and the Roman concept of property remains fundamental to legal systems everywhere. The Romans developed a clear and powerful idea of ownership, which they called dominium, meaning the full and absolute right of a person over a thing. Ownership, in the Roman conception, was the most complete right a person could have over property, encompassing the right to use it, to enjoy its fruits and benefits, and to dispose of it as the owner wished, including by selling it, giving it away, or destroying it. This idea of ownership as a comprehensive and exclusive right over a thing became the foundation of property law in the Western tradition and remains central to how we understand property today.

The Romans distinguished carefully between ownership and mere possession, and this distinction, subtle but essential, shows the analytical sophistication of Roman legal thought. Ownership is the right to a thing, the legal entitlement to it, while possession is the actual physical control of a thing, the fact of holding it, regardless of whether one has the right to it. A thief, for example, has possession of the stolen goods but not ownership, while the true owner retains ownership even though he's lost possession. This distinction between the right to a thing and the physical control of it allowed the Romans to develop nuanced rules about property, protecting both the rights of owners and the interests of those in actual possession, and it remains a basic distinction in property law to this day. The Romans also worked out detailed rules about how ownership could be acquired and transferred, about rights that one person could have over another's property, such as rights of way and other servitudes, and about the many other complexities of property relationships, building a body of property law of remarkable sophistication.

Contract was another area of profound Roman achievement, and the Roman law of contract lies at the foundation of contract law throughout the world. The Romans developed a sophisticated understanding of contracts as agreements that create legally binding obligations, and they worked out detailed rules governing the many different kinds of agreements that people make. They recognized various types of contracts, each with its own rules, covering sale, hire, loan, partnership, deposit, and other common transactions, and they analyzed with great care the obligations that each kind of contract created, the duties of the parties, and the consequences of failing to perform. This detailed and systematic law of contract gave Roman commerce a reliable legal framework and provided the model for contract law in later legal systems.

The Romans thought deeply about what made a contract valid and binding, examining questions that remain central to contract law today. They considered the importance of the agreement of the parties, the meeting of minds that lies at the heart of a contract, and they grappled with problems like the effect of mistake, fraud, and duress on the validity of an agreement.

If a person entered a contract under a serious mistake about what they were agreeing to, or because they'd been deceived, or because they'd been coerced by threats, did the contract still bind them? The Romans worked through these questions with characteristic care, developing rules that balanced the need to hold people to their agreements against the recognition that some agreements shouldn't be enforced because of the circumstances in which they were made. These questions, and the sophisticated answers the Romans gave to them, remain at the center of contract law in every modern legal system.

The third great area was the law of wrongs, what we would now call tort, the branch of law dealing with harms that one person wrongfully causes to another outside of any contract between them. The Romans developed rules governing liability for wrongful harm, working out when a person who caused injury or damage to another should be legally responsible for it and required to compensate the victim. A key concept in this area was the idea of fault, the notion that a person should generally be held liable for harm they caused through their wrongful conduct, whether through a deliberate wrong or through carelessness. This idea of fault-based liability, that responsibility for harm should generally rest on wrongful conduct rather than on the mere fact of having caused harm, became fundamental to the law of tort and remains central to it today.

An important Roman law in this area was the Lex Aquilia, a statute concerning damage to property that became the foundation for much of the later development of the law of wrongful harm. The Lex Aquilia provided compensation for wrongful damage to another's property, such as the killing or injuring of another person's slaves or animals, or damage to their goods, and the Roman jurists interpreted and extended it over time to cover an increasingly wide range of situations. Through their analysis of the Lex Aquilia and related rules, the jurists developed a sophisticated body of law about liability for wrongful harm, exploring questions about causation, about the degree of fault required for liability, and about the measure of compensation owed, questions that remain central to the law of tort in modern legal systems. The Roman law of wrongful harm, growing out of the Lex Aquilia and the jurists' interpretation of it, became the ancestor of the modern law of negligence and tort.

The table below shows the three foundational areas of Roman private law and the core concepts the Romans developed in each.

Area	Roman Concept	Core Principle	Modern Descendant
Property	Dominium (ownership)	Full, exclusive right over a thing, distinct from possession	Property law
Contract	Binding agreement	Agreements create enforceable obligations	Contract law
Wrongful harm	Fault-based liability	Responsibility rests on wrongful conduct	Tort and negligence law

What unites these three areas, and what makes them so important, is the precision and the analytical quality of the Roman legal thinking behind them. The Roman jurists didn't just make rules; they developed concepts, clear and carefully defined categories that allowed the law to handle complex situations in a rational and consistent way.

The distinction between ownership and possession, the analysis of different types of contracts and the obligations they create, the idea of fault-based liability for wrongful harm, these are conceptual tools of great power and refinement, and they've proven so useful that they remain the basic apparatus of private law across the world. When modern lawyers reason about who owns what, about whether a contract is binding, or about who's liable for an injury, they're using categories and concepts that Roman jurists worked out two thousand years ago. This is the deepest reason for the lasting influence of Roman law: not merely that it was preserved and transmitted, but that the law itself was so well-made that it has never been surpassed as a foundation for the private law of civilized societies.

The spread of Roman law across conquered territories

Roman law didn't remain confined to the city of Rome or even to Italy. As Rome expanded to rule an empire encompassing much of Europe, North Africa, and the Middle East, its law spread across these vast territories, and the mechanisms by which Roman law extended across the conquered lands, and the ways it interacted with the laws of the peoples Rome absorbed, form an important part of the story of Roman law and its lasting influence. The spread of Roman law across the empire helped lay the foundation for its later role as the common legal inheritance of much of the Western world.

In the early period, Roman law had applied only to Roman citizens. Citizenship was a privileged status, and the civil law of Rome, the ius civile, was the law of the citizens, governing their relationships and transactions among themselves. The many non-citizens living within the empire's expanding borders, the conquered and incorporated peoples who didn't hold Roman citizenship, weren't governed by the ius civile and continued in many respects to live under their own local laws and customs. This created a practical problem as Rome's territory and commerce grew, because the Romans increasingly interacted and did business with non-citizens, and disputes arose that the citizens-only ius civile wasn't designed to handle.

To address this, the Romans developed a body of law called the ius gentium, the "law of nations" or "law of peoples," and this development had significance far beyond its immediate practical purpose. The ius gentium was the law that the Romans applied in dealings involving non-citizens, and in disputes between Romans and foreigners or between foreigners of different origins. It grew out of the practical need to handle the affairs of the diverse peoples of the empire, and it consisted of legal principles that the Romans regarded as common to all peoples, rules based on natural reason and good faith that seemed to hold generally rather than being peculiar to Roman citizens alone. The ius gentium tended to be more flexible and less formal than the old ius civile, and it proved well-suited to the practical needs of commerce among the varied peoples of the empire.

The concept of the ius gentium connected with the philosophical idea of natural law that the Greeks, and especially the Stoics, had developed. The Romans came to associate the ius gentium, the law common to all peoples, with the idea of a natural law grounded in reason and common to all humanity, a law that reflected principles of justice valid everywhere rather than the particular customs of one people. This connection between the practical law of nations and the philosophical idea of natural law was important, and it fed into the later development of legal thought, contributing to ideas about a universal law binding on all peoples that would prove influential for centuries, eventually informing the development of international law and the idea of universal human rights.

A momentous change came in 212 CE, when the emperor Caracalla issued an edict, known as the Constitutio Antoniniana, granting Roman citizenship to nearly all free inhabitants of the empire. At a stroke, this extended Roman citizenship, and with it the application of Roman law, to the vast population of the empire who'd previously been non-citizens. The effect was to make Roman law the common law of essentially the entire free population of the Roman world, spreading it across the whole empire as the law of all its citizens. This universal extension of Roman citizenship and Roman law helped establish Roman law as the shared legal inheritance of the many peoples the empire had brought together, an inheritance that would outlast the empire itself.

The spread of Roman law across the empire had lasting consequences that reached far beyond the empire's own lifetime, and this is what makes it so significant for the broader history of law. In the lands that had been part of the Roman Empire, Roman law left a deep and enduring mark, shaping the legal customs and traditions of the regions long after Roman political control had ended. When the western empire fell and the Germanic kingdoms arose on its former territory, Roman law wasn't vanquished, but persisted in various forms among the Roman population, influenced the laws of the Germanic rulers, and remained part of the legal fabric of these lands. Later, when the study of Roman law revived in medieval Europe through the rediscovery of Justinian's compilation, it found fertile ground precisely in these regions that had once been Roman and that retained the traces of their Roman legal heritage.

Through this long history, the spread of Roman law across the ancient empire helped make it the common foundation of the Western legal tradition. The regions of continental Europe that had been part of the Roman Empire developed legal systems built on the foundation of Roman law, and as European powers later extended their influence across the globe, they carried this Roman-based law with them to the many parts of the world that came under European rule or influence.

This is why Roman law, though it originated in a single ancient city, became the foundation of the legal systems of a large part of the modern world, governing the private law of continental Europe, Latin America, and many other regions to this day. The law that Rome spread across its empire two thousand years ago became, through the long processes of history, one of the great foundations of law across the modern world, a legacy that far outlasted the empire that first created and spread it.

Discussion question: Roman law achieved its lasting power largely through the work of jurists who developed the law gradually through expert interpretation rather than through legislatures passing statutes, yet modern democracies generally insist that law should be made by elected representatives accountable to the people. Is there something valuable in the Roman model of law developed by legal experts reasoning from principle, something that democratic lawmaking by legislation might lack, or does the Roman approach place too much power in the hands of an unelected elite, however skilled?

Chapter 5: Law in the Ancient Near East and Asia

So far, much of our story has followed a line that leads toward the Western legal tradition, from Mesopotamia through Greece and Rome. But law developed across the whole of the ancient world, and some of the richest and most sophisticated legal traditions grew up far from the Mediterranean, in societies with their own distinct ideas about justice, order, and the proper relationship between people and the law. These traditions deserve attention both in their own right and because they show us something important: that there was no single path to law, no one way of answering the questions that every complex society must confront. Different civilizations, working independently, arrived at strikingly different answers.

This chapter turns to the legal traditions of the ancient Near East beyond Babylon and to the great legal cultures of India and China. In these societies we find approaches to law that differ profoundly from one another and from the Western tradition, revealing the remarkable variety of ways that humans have organized justice and order.

We'll see a society that gave us some of the harshest surviving ancient laws alongside real protections for women's property. We'll encounter an ancient Indian masterwork of statecraft that treated law as an instrument of royal power and practical governance. We'll examine the great debate in ancient China between two opposed visions of how society should be governed. And we'll look at a system that bound legal obligation tightly to a rigid hierarchy of social rank.

What these traditions share, despite their differences, is that each grappled seriously with the fundamental problems of law: how to maintain order, how to resolve disputes, how to define people's rights and duties, and how to relate law to the deeper values of the society. And each arrived at answers shaped by its own circumstances, its own beliefs, and its own understanding of the world.

Studying them broadens our sense of what law is and can be, showing that the legal ideas we might take for granted are not the only possibilities, but particular choices among many that human societies have made.

Assyrian law and its treatment of women and property

The Assyrians built one of the great empires of the ancient Near East, a powerful and often feared civilization centered in northern Mesopotamia. They've left us a body of law preserved on clay tablets, the Middle Assyrian Laws, dating to around the fourteenth to eleventh centuries BCE, and these laws offer a fascinating and sometimes disturbing window into Assyrian society. They're notable for two things in particular: the severity of their punishments, which were harsh even by the standards of the ancient world, and their detailed treatment of matters concerning women, marriage, and property, which reveals a great deal about the position of women in Assyrian society.

The Middle Assyrian Laws were considerably more severe than the earlier Babylonian codes we've examined. Where Hammurabi's code had relied heavily on the talion, the eye for an eye, and on monetary compensation, the Assyrian laws prescribed brutal physical punishments for a wide range of offenses, including beatings, mutilation, and various forms of bodily harm inflicted as penalties. Floggings of specified numbers of blows, the cutting off of ears, noses, fingers, or lips, and other mutilations appear as punishments in the Assyrian laws, often combined with periods of forced labor for the king. This harshness reflects something of the character of Assyrian civilization, which was known for its military power and for a certain severity in its methods, and it stands as a reminder that the trend of legal history was not a steady movement toward greater gentleness but varied enormously from one society to another.

The Assyrian laws are especially known for a group of provisions dealing with women, and these provisions have attracted particular attention because of what they reveal about the position of women in Assyrian society and about the ways that ancient law regulated women's lives and bodies. The laws concerning women in the Middle Assyrian collection are extensive and detailed, addressing marriage, divorce, inheritance, sexual offenses, and the conduct and status of women in considerable depth, and they paint a picture of a society that placed women under significant legal restrictions and subjected them to the control of men, whether fathers or husbands.

The Assyrian laws show us a society in which women's lives were closely regulated and in which women were, in many respects, under the authority and control of the men of their families. The laws governed a woman's transition from the control of her father to the control of her husband through marriage, and they subjected women to various restrictions and to penalties for offenses that often fell more heavily on women than on men. One notable provision required certain classes of women to be veiled in public while prohibiting others, such as slaves and certain other women, from veiling, using the veil as a marker of a woman's status and imposing punishments on those who violated the rules about who could and couldn't be veiled. Provisions of this kind reveal a society deeply concerned with regulating women according to their status and with maintaining sharp distinctions between different categories of women.

Yet alongside these restrictions, the Assyrian laws also recognized certain property rights for women, and this is where the picture becomes more complicated and more interesting than a simple story of oppression. Assyrian women could hold property in various forms, and the laws addressed women's property, including the property a woman brought into her marriage and property she might receive or inherit. A married woman had certain rights regarding her dowry and other property associated with her, and the laws protected these property interests in various circumstances, such as in the event of her husband's death or in cases of divorce. So while Assyrian women lived under significant legal restrictions and male control, they weren't entirely without legal standing or property rights, and the law recognized and protected certain interests of women even within a system that subordinated them in many other ways.

This combination, of harsh restriction on the one hand and recognition of certain property rights on the other, illustrates something important about the position of women in ancient law generally. The situation of women in ancient legal systems was often complex and can't be reduced to a simple picture of complete subordination or complete lack of rights. Women lived under real restrictions and under the authority of men in most ancient societies, but they also frequently possessed certain legal rights, particularly regarding property, that gave them a real if limited legal standing. The Assyrian laws capture this complexity vividly, showing a society that subjected women to severe restrictions and control while nonetheless recognizing and protecting certain of their property interests. Understanding the position of women in ancient law requires holding both of these realities together, seeing both the restrictions and the rights, and recognizing that the legal situation of women was often a matter of limited and qualified standing within systems that were fundamentally organized around male authority.

Arthashastra: statecraft and law in ancient India

Ancient India produced one of the most remarkable works on government, politics, and law in all of human history, a treatise called the Arthashastra. Attributed to a minister and adviser named Kautilya, also known as Chanakya, who is traditionally associated with the founding of the Maurya Empire in the late fourth century BCE, the Arthashastra is a comprehensive manual of statecraft, covering the practical arts of governing a state, and it includes extensive treatment of law and justice as essential elements of effective government. It's a work of extraordinary sophistication and hard-headed practicality, and it offers a distinctive vision of law as an instrument of statecraft and royal power.

The Arthashastra takes a thoroughly practical and unsentimental approach to government and law, concerning itself with what actually works to maintain and strengthen the power of the state rather than with abstract ideals of justice. It's often compared to the later work of the Italian political thinker Machiavelli for its realistic, sometimes ruthless, approach to the exercise of power, though the Arthashastra is far more comprehensive, covering the whole business of governing a state in exhaustive detail. It addresses the organization of government, the management of the economy, the conduct of war and diplomacy, the gathering of intelligence, the administration of justice, and countless other aspects of statecraft, all with a keen eye to the practical realities of maintaining and expanding royal power.

In the Arthashastra, law appears as a means of governance and an instrument of the king's authority. The maintenance of order and the administration of justice are treated as essential functions of the state, necessary for the security and prosperity of the kingdom and for the maintenance of royal power.

The treatise sets out detailed provisions concerning law and legal administration, covering the courts, legal procedure, the different types of legal disputes, and the substance of the law across a wide range of areas including contracts, property, debt, marriage, inheritance, and criminal offenses. This body of law is presented as part of the machinery of the state, a means by which the king maintains order, resolves disputes, and controls his kingdom.

The Arthashastra recognizes several sources of law and addresses how they relate to one another, showing a sophisticated understanding of the different foundations on which law could rest. It acknowledges sacred law rooted in religious tradition, along with custom, the evidence and conduct of the parties, and, importantly, royal decree, the edicts and commands of the king. And notably, the Arthashastra gives great weight to royal authority in the making and administration of law, reflecting its overall emphasis on the power of the state and the king. In cases of conflict between different sources of law, the treatise tends to elevate royal command and practical considerations of statecraft, treating the king's law as a powerful force in the legal order. This emphasis on royal authority as a central source of law reflects the Arthashastra's broader vision of a strong, centralized state in which the king holds extensive power over the affairs of the kingdom, including its law.

The legal provisions of the Arthashastra are remarkably detailed and practical, covering an enormous range of situations with the same thoroughness the treatise brings to every subject. It addresses the formation and enforcement of contracts, the rules governing loans and debts and the rates of interest, the law of property and its transfer, the regulation of various trades and transactions, the handling of disputes between partners and among family members, and a wide array of criminal offenses and their punishments. It sets out procedures for the conduct of legal cases, rules of evidence, and the organization of the courts, providing a comprehensive framework for the administration of justice. The level of detail and practical concern in these provisions reflects the Arthashastra's character as a working manual of government, intended to guide the actual administration of a real kingdom rather than to explore abstract questions of legal philosophy.

The Arthashastra also reveals a state deeply concerned with surveillance, control, and the gathering of information, and this dimension of the work is striking and somewhat unsettling to modern readers. The treatise describes an extensive system of spies and informants used by the king to monitor his officials, his subjects, and potential threats to his power, treating the gathering of intelligence and the surveillance of the population as essential tools of statecraft. This concern with control and surveillance extends to the legal and administrative system, which is designed in part to give the king detailed knowledge of and control over the affairs of his kingdom. The Arthashastra presents a vision of a powerful, centralized, and intrusive state that monitors and controls its subjects closely, using law and administration as instruments of royal power and control. This vision reflects a distinctive understanding of the relationship between the state and its subjects, one that emphasizes the power of the state and the subordination of the population to royal authority.

For all its hard-headed emphasis on power and control, the Arthashastra also reflects a genuine concern with the welfare of the kingdom and with the effective and orderly administration of justice, and it would be a mistake to see it as merely a manual of ruthless power. The treatise recognizes that a well-governed kingdom, with a fair and effective legal system, is more secure, more prosperous, and more stable than a poorly governed one, and it treats good governance, including sound administration of justice, as being in the king's own interest. The Arthashastra advises the king to be attentive to the welfare of his subjects, to administer justice fairly and effectively, and to maintain order and prosperity in the kingdom, recognizing that the strength and security of the state depend on good governance.

So while the Arthashastra takes a practical and power-centered approach to law and government, it also reflects an understanding that effective and reasonably fair administration serves the interests of the state, blending a realistic concern with power and a genuine concern with sound and orderly governance.

Legalism versus Confucianism in early Chinese legal thought

Ancient China developed one of the world's great legal and philosophical traditions, and at the heart of early Chinese thinking about law lay a profound debate between two opposed visions of how society should be governed and ordered. These two visions, associated with the schools of thought known as Legalism and Confucianism, offered fundamentally different answers to the question of how to achieve social order and good government, and their long contest shaped Chinese law and government for over two thousand years. Understanding this debate is essential to understanding not only Chinese law but the broader question of the relationship between law, morality, and social order that lies at the heart of legal philosophy everywhere.

(Confucius shaped early Chinese legal thought by emphasizing **li**, i.e., moral ritual order and social duty, so law was seen less as punishment and more as a way to preserve harmony through virtue and proper relationships.)

Confucianism, the tradition of thought associated with the great teacher Confucius, who lived in the sixth and fifth centuries BCE, and his followers, held that social order should be achieved primarily through morality, virtue, and proper relationships rather than through law and punishment. The Confucian vision emphasized the cultivation of moral character, the observance of proper social relationships and rituals, and the leadership of virtuous rulers who would guide society by their moral example. For the Confucians, the ideal way to achieve social order was through the moral transformation of people, through education and the cultivation of virtue, so that people would behave well because they'd internalized proper moral values and understood their proper roles and relationships, not because they feared punishment.

The Confucians were deeply skeptical of relying on law and punishment to maintain order, and this skepticism was central to their view. They held that governing through strict laws and harsh punishments was inferior to governing through virtue and moral example, and that a society ordered primarily by fear of punishment would be inferior to one ordered by moral cultivation.

Confucius himself taught that if people are led by laws and kept in order by punishments, they'll seek to avoid the punishment but will have no sense of shame, whereas if they're led by virtue and kept in order by proper social conduct, they'll develop a sense of shame and will become good. The Confucian ideal was a society in which people behaved well out of genuine virtue and a sense of what was proper, guided by the moral example of their rulers and by the observance of proper relationships and rituals, rather than a society held in line by the threat of legal punishment.

Legalism, by contrast, took a diametrically opposed view, holding that social order could be achieved only through strict laws, clear rewards and punishments, and the firm authority of the state. The Legalists, whose most important thinker was Han Feizi in the third century BCE, were deeply skeptical of the Confucian reliance on morality and virtue, believing that human nature was fundamentally selfish and that people couldn't be relied upon to behave well of their own accord. For the Legalists, the only reliable way to achieve social order was through a system of clear, strict laws, uniformly applied, backed by rewards for obedience and severe punishments for disobedience. People would behave well, in the Legalist view, not because they were virtuous but because the law made it clearly in their interest to do so, rewarding compliance and punishing violation with certainty and severity.

The Legalists emphasized several principles that gave their philosophy its distinctive character. They held that the law should be clear, publicly known, and uniformly applied to everyone, so that people would know exactly what was required and what the consequences of violation would be. They emphasized that punishments should be severe and certain, so that people would be deterred from wrongdoing by the sure knowledge that violation would bring harsh penalties. And they insisted that the law should apply equally to all, regardless of rank or status, so that the law's authority would be absolute and its application uniform, though the ruler himself stood above and behind the law as its source. The Legalist vision was of a powerful, centralized state maintaining strict order through a system of clear laws and severe punishments, uniformly and impartially applied, with the authority of the state standing behind the whole system.

The contest between these two philosophies had enormous practical consequences for Chinese history. Legalism provided the philosophy behind the Qin dynasty, which unified China for the first time in 221 BCE under the First Emperor. The Qin state adopted Legalist principles, building a powerful, centralized government that maintained order through strict laws and severe punishments, and this Legalist approach helped the Qin conquer the other states and unify China under a single rule. But the harshness of the Qin regime, with its severe laws and brutal punishments, generated deep resentment, and the Qin dynasty collapsed shortly after the death of the First Emperor, having lasted only about fifteen years. The rapid fall of the Qin, associated with the harshness of its Legalist methods, discredited Legalism in its pure form and became a lesson in the dangers of governing through severity alone.

The dynasty that followed, the Han, adopted Confucianism as its official philosophy, and this marked a turning point in Chinese history whose effects lasted for two millennia. But in practice, Chinese government and law came to combine elements of both traditions, and this blending is one of the most important facts about the Chinese legal tradition. Although Confucianism became the dominant official philosophy, providing the moral and ideological foundation of the state, the actual administration of government and law continued to make use of laws and punishments in the Legalist manner. The result was a synthesis, often described as Confucianism on the outside and Legalism on the inside, in which the moral principles of Confucianism provided the official framework and ideal while the practical tools of Legalism, laws and punishments, continued to be used in the actual governance of the state. This blending of Confucian morality and Legalist method characterized Chinese law and government for the following two thousand years, shaping one of the world's great and enduring legal traditions.

Below we set the two philosophies side by side, showing how fundamentally they differed in their view of human nature and their prescription for social order.

	Confucianism	**Legalism**
View of human nature	People can be made good through cultivation	People are fundamentally selfish
Basis of social order	Morality, virtue, proper relationships	Strict laws, rewards, and punishments
Role of law	Secondary to moral example	Primary and essential
Attitude to punishment	Inferior to moral guidance	Necessary, severe, and certain
Ideal ruler	A virtuous moral example	A firm authority behind the law
Historical association	The Han dynasty and after	The Qin dynasty

The Chinese debate between Legalism and Confucianism illuminates a question that runs through the history of law everywhere: the question of the proper relationship between law and morality, and of whether social order is best achieved through law and punishment or through the cultivation of virtue and proper values. The Confucians and Legalists gave opposed answers to this question, and the enduring Chinese synthesis of the two reflects a recognition that both may have something to offer, that a well-ordered society may need both the moral foundation the Confucians emphasized and the practical tools of law and punishment the Legalists insisted upon. This ancient Chinese debate, and the synthesis that emerged from it, represents one of the most profound explorations of the relationship between law and morality in the history of human thought, and its central question remains alive in every society that must decide how far to rely on law and how far on shared values in maintaining social order.

The Laws of Manu and caste-based legal obligation

The Laws of Manu, known in Sanskrit as the Manusmriti, is one of the most important legal and religious texts of ancient India, a work that had a profound and lasting influence on Indian society and law. Composed over a period ending in roughly the early centuries of the common era, the Laws of Manu is a comprehensive treatise on law, duty, and proper conduct, setting out an elaborate system of social and legal obligations governing nearly every aspect of life. Its most distinctive and consequential feature is the way it tied legal and social obligation to the system of caste, the hierarchical division of society into ranked groups, making a person's duties, rights, and legal treatment depend heavily on their place in the caste hierarchy.

To understand the Laws of Manu, we need to understand the concept that lies at its heart: the idea of dharma. Dharma is a rich and complex concept in Indian thought, encompassing law, duty, righteousness, and the proper order of things, and it refers to the moral and social duties appropriate to a person according to their place in the social order and their stage of life. The Laws of Manu is fundamentally concerned with dharma, with setting out the proper duties and conduct appropriate to different people in different circumstances, and it presents an elaborate system of obligations tied to a person's caste, their occupation, their stage of life, and their particular situation. In this conception, law and duty aren't the same for everyone but vary according to who a person is and what their place in the social order requires of them.

The caste system that the Laws of Manu reflects and reinforces divided society into four main groups, arranged in a hierarchy. At the top were the Brahmins, the priests and scholars, followed by the Kshatriyas, the warriors and rulers, then the Vaishyas, the merchants, farmers, and traders, and finally the Shudras, the laborers and servants.

Below and outside this fourfold hierarchy were those regarded as untouchables, considered to fall outside the caste system altogether and subjected to severe social exclusion and disability. The Laws of Manu treated this hierarchical division of society as the fundamental structure of the social and moral order, and it made a person's duties, rights, and legal treatment depend heavily on their place within it.

The consequences of this caste-based approach to law were far-reaching, because the Laws of Manu prescribed different duties, different rights, and different legal treatment for people of different castes. The obligations appropriate to a Brahmin differed from those appropriate to a Kshatriya, a Vaishya, or a Shudra, and the text set out in detail the proper conduct, occupations, and duties for each group. Legal treatment, too, varied by caste, and this is where the system's inequality became most stark. The same offense might carry very different consequences depending on the caste of the offender and the caste of the victim, with punishments often more severe for those of lower caste and penalties for offenses against higher-caste persons typically greater than for the same offenses against those of lower caste. A person's caste profoundly affected their legal position, their rights, and the way the law treated them, making caste a central factor in the legal order.

The Laws of Manu addressed an enormous range of subjects beyond the basic structure of caste obligation, presenting a comprehensive vision of proper life and conduct. It covered the duties of the different castes and the different stages of life, the conduct of rulers and the administration of justice, marriage and family relationships, inheritance and property, various offenses and their punishments, religious duties and rituals, and countless matters of daily conduct and proper behavior. It set out an elaborate framework of duty and obligation touching nearly every aspect of life, all organized around the fundamental principle that duty and proper conduct varied according to a person's place in the social order. In this way, the Laws of Manu presented not just a legal code in the narrow sense but a total vision of proper social and moral order, in which law, religion, duty, and social hierarchy were woven together into a single comprehensive system.

The influence of the Laws of Manu on Indian society was profound and long-lasting, shaping Indian social and legal thought for many centuries and helping entrench the caste system as a fundamental feature of Indian society. The text became a central authority in the Hindu legal and social tradition, and its vision of a hierarchically ordered society with duties and rights tied to caste deeply influenced the actual organization of Indian society over a long period.

This influence had enduring consequences, and the caste system that the Laws of Manu reflected and reinforced remained a powerful force in Indian society for a very long time, with effects that persisted into the modern era. It's worth noting that modern India has formally abolished caste discrimination, with the Constitution of independent India prohibiting untouchability and discrimination on the basis of caste, marking a decisive legal rejection of the caste-based inequality that the Laws of Manu had embodied. But for many centuries, the Laws of Manu and the caste-based vision of law and society it represented exercised a profound influence on Indian life.

The Laws of Manu presents a striking contrast to some of the ideas we've encountered elsewhere, and this contrast is illuminating for our understanding of the range of possibilities in the history of law. Where the Stoic philosophers of the Greek and Roman world had developed the idea of a natural law common to all humanity and of a fundamental equality among all people by virtue of their shared rational nature, the Laws of Manu presented a vision of law and duty fundamentally structured by hierarchy and difference, in which people's duties, rights, and legal treatment varied profoundly according to their place in the social order. These represent two very different visions of the foundation of law and justice: one grounded in a common humanity and a universal law applying equally to all, the other grounded in hierarchy and difference, with duty and law varying according to social rank. The contrast between these visions illustrates the profound variety in the ways that human societies have understood the foundations of law and justice, and it reminds us that the idea of equality before the law, which we might take for granted, was by no means universal in the ancient world but was one particular vision among several very different ones. Studying a tradition like the Laws of Manu, so different in its assumptions from the ideas that shaped the Western legal tradition, deepens our appreciation of just how varied the human approaches to law have been, and of how the fundamental assumptions of a legal system, about equality or hierarchy, about whether law is the same for all or varies by status, shape the entire character of that system and the society it governs.

Discussion question: The traditions in this chapter tied law to social hierarchy in ways the modern world has largely rejected, yet each of these societies maintained order and endured for centuries under systems that treated people unequally by design. If a legal system that openly ranks people can still function and last, what does that tell us about the relationship between a legal system's justice and its stability, and should we conclude that the fairness of a legal order and its ability to endure are separate questions entirely?

Chapter 6: Medieval European Legal Systems

When the western Roman Empire collapsed in the fifth century, the sophisticated legal machinery that had governed the Mediterranean world for centuries broke down with it. The professional jurists, the great compilations, the unified system of law administered across a vast territory, all of this faded as Germanic peoples established new kingdoms on the ruins of Roman rule. For a time it might have seemed that the achievement of Roman law would be lost entirely, dissolved into the simpler customs of the warrior peoples who now held power. But law didn't disappear from Europe. It took new forms, drew on new sources, and over the medieval centuries developed into systems that would prove enormously important for the future.

Medieval Europe was a patchwork of overlapping authorities and competing sources of law, and this is the first thing to understand about it. There was no single legal system, no unified state administering one body of law across the continent. Instead there were multiple, overlapping legal orders operating side by side, sometimes cooperating and sometimes clashing.

The Catholic Church had its own law, canon law, which governed a wide range of matters across all of Christendom. The feudal system generated its own law of lords and vassals, of land and personal obligation. Kings issued their own laws and built their own courts. Towns had their own customs and privileges. Merchants developed their own law for trade. And older Roman law survived in various forms, especially in the south, waiting to be revived. This complex, layered, and often competing arrangement of legal authorities is characteristic of the medieval period and quite different from the unified legal systems we know today.

Out of this complex medieval world came developments of lasting importance for the history of law. The revival of Roman law transformed European legal thought and laid the foundation for the civil law tradition of the continent. The struggle to place limits on royal power produced documents and principles that would shape the development of constitutional government.

And in England, a distinctive legal system took shape, the common law, which would eventually spread across much of the world and become one of the two great legal traditions of the modern age. This chapter explores these medieval developments, tracing how law rebuilt itself after the fall of Rome and set the stage for the legal systems of the modern world.

Canon law and the authority of the Catholic Church

In medieval Europe, the Catholic Church was not merely a religious institution but one of the most powerful legal and political forces in the whole of society. The Church had its own comprehensive system of law, known as canon law, which governed a wide range of matters and applied throughout the whole of Western Christendom, across the boundaries of the many kingdoms and territories into which medieval Europe was divided. Canon law was one of the most sophisticated and influential legal systems of the medieval period, and understanding it is essential to understanding medieval law as a whole, because the Church's law reached into the lives of ordinary people in ways that touched some of their most important concerns.

Canon law derived from several sources, and the way these sources were gathered and organized became a major intellectual achievement of the medieval period. It drew on the scriptures, the writings of the early Church fathers, the decisions of Church councils, the decrees of popes, and other authoritative sources of Christian teaching and Church regulation. Over the centuries, this body of religious and ecclesiastical law accumulated into a large and complex mass of material, and a crucial step in its development came in the twelfth century when a scholar named Gratian produced a systematic compilation and analysis of canon law, a work commonly known as the Decretum. Gratian's Decretum brought order and system to the sprawling body of canon law, reconciling apparent contradictions and organizing the material into a coherent whole, and it became the foundation for the study and development of canon law as a sophisticated legal science, much as Justinian's compilation had done for Roman law.

The jurisdiction of canon law was remarkably broad, extending well beyond what we might think of as purely religious matters and reaching into areas of great practical importance in people's daily lives. The Church's courts had authority over a wide range of subjects, and this authority made canon law a significant force in the everyday life of medieval Europeans. Canon law governed matters concerning the clergy and the internal affairs of the Church, as we'd expect, but it also extended its reach much further, into areas that affected the lives of ordinary lay people in fundamental ways.

Among the most important areas of canon law jurisdiction was marriage, which the Church regarded as a sacrament and which fell under the authority of canon law and the Church's courts. The Church developed an elaborate body of law governing marriage, addressing what made a valid marriage, who could marry whom, the requirements for a lawful union, and questions concerning the validity or annulment of marriages. Because marriage was central to family life, property, inheritance, and social relationships, the Church's control over marriage law gave it enormous influence over some of the most important matters in people's lives. The Church's marriage law shaped the family life of medieval Europe and established principles, such as the requirement of consent for a valid marriage, that had lasting importance. This principle that a marriage required the genuine consent of both parties was significant, and it reflected and reinforced the idea that marriage was based on the agreement of the two people entering it.

Canon law also governed a range of other important matters, extending the Church's legal authority across a broad swath of medieval life. It had authority over wills and the disposition of property after death in many circumstances, giving the Church a significant role in matters of inheritance. It governed various matters concerning oaths and promises made under religious sanction, and it had jurisdiction over a range of moral offenses and matters touching on sin and religious duty. The

Church's courts heard cases in all these areas, applying canon law and exercising a legal authority that reached deep into the lives of ordinary people. The Church could also impose serious penalties, including excommunication, the exclusion of a person from the community of the Church and its sacraments, which was a grave penalty in a deeply religious society and gave the Church's law real force.

Canon law was administered through a system of Church courts that operated throughout medieval Europe, forming an organized judicial hierarchy that paralleled the structure of the Church itself. These ecclesiastical courts existed at various levels, from local Church courts up through higher courts, with the papal court in Rome at the summit as the highest authority in the Church's legal system. This meant that canon law functioned as an international legal system, applying across the whole of Western Christendom and administered through an organized hierarchy of courts that transcended the boundaries of the individual kingdoms and territories of medieval Europe. In this respect, canon law was unique among the legal systems of the medieval period, being the one body of law that applied universally across Western Christendom rather than being confined to a particular kingdom or locality, which gave it a reach and a unifying influence that no secular law of the period possessed.

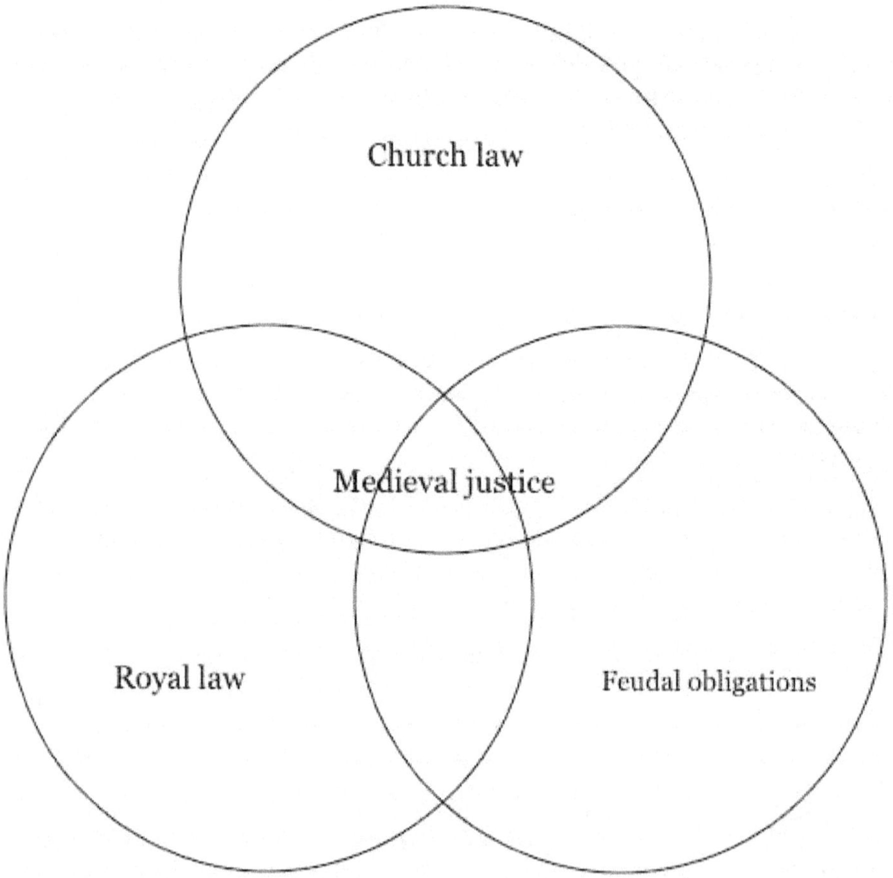

The relationship between canon law and the secular legal authorities of medieval Europe was complex and often marked by tension and conflict. The Church claimed authority over a wide range of matters, and its claims sometimes clashed with the claims of kings and other secular rulers who had their own courts and their own law. Disputes over the boundaries between Church and secular jurisdiction, over which matters fell under the authority of the Church's courts and which under the secular courts, were a recurring feature of medieval legal and political life, and these disputes were part of the broader struggle between Church and state that ran through the medieval period.

The competition between the authority of the Church and the authority of secular rulers, including competition over legal jurisdiction, was one of the defining features of medieval European politics, and it had lasting consequences for the development of law and government in Europe, contributing in the long run to ideas about the limits of different kinds of authority and the separation of different spheres of power.

Feudal law and the obligations of lords and serfs

Feudalism was the characteristic social, political, and economic system of much of medieval Europe, and it generated its own distinctive body of law, feudal law, which governed the relationships and obligations at the heart of the feudal order.

Understanding feudal law requires understanding the feudal system itself, a system built around relationships of personal loyalty and obligation, and around the holding of land in exchange for service. Feudal law was the law of these relationships and obligations, and it shaped the lives of nearly everyone in medieval Europe, from the greatest lords to the humblest peasants.

At the heart of the feudal system was a relationship between a lord and a vassal, and this relationship was fundamentally a legal one, defined by mutual obligations that bound the two parties together. The lord granted the vassal the use of land, called a fief, and in return the vassal owed the lord various services and obligations, most importantly military service. The vassal swore an oath of loyalty to the lord and became the lord's man, bound to serve and support him, while the lord in turn owed the vassal protection and the maintenance of his rights in the fief. This relationship was reciprocal, involving obligations on both sides, and it was understood in legal terms, with defined duties that each party owed the other and with consequences for failing to fulfill those duties.

The feudal relationship was structured around the holding of land, and this connection between land and personal obligation was central to the whole feudal order. The fief, the land granted by the lord to the vassal, was the material basis of the relationship, and the vassal's obligations were tied to his holding of the fief. The vassal held the land not as absolute owner in the way we might think of ownership today, but on condition of fulfilling the obligations he owed to his lord, and the land could revert to the lord in certain circumstances, such as the vassal's failure to fulfill his obligations or the vassal's death without a proper heir. This conditional holding of land in exchange for service was the essential feature of the feudal system, tying together land, personal loyalty, and mutual obligation into a single relationship governed by feudal law.

Feudal society was arranged in a hierarchy of these lord-vassal relationships, forming a chain of obligations that ran through the whole of society. A great lord might be the vassal of the king, holding land from the king in exchange for service, while himself being the lord of lesser vassals who held land from him in exchange for their service, and so on down through the levels of society. This created a complex web of relationships in which a person might be both a vassal to those above him and a lord to those below him, with obligations running in both directions.

The king stood at the top of this hierarchy, at least in theory, as the ultimate source of the land held throughout the kingdom, though in practice the power of medieval kings was often limited and the great lords could be very powerful in their own right. This hierarchical structure of feudal relationships, with its chains of obligation running through society, was the basic framework of medieval political and social organization.

Feudal law developed detailed rules governing the relationships and obligations of the feudal system, addressing the many questions that arose in the working of the feudal order. It governed the granting and holding of fiefs, the obligations owed by vassals to lords and by lords to vassals, the inheritance of fiefs, the circumstances in which a fief might revert to the lord, and the resolution of disputes between lords and vassals. Feudal law also addressed the various dues and services that were owed within the feudal system, the aids and payments that vassals owed their lords in certain circumstances, and the rights that lords had over their vassals and their fiefs. This body of feudal law was often administered in the courts of the lords, where disputes concerning feudal relationships and obligations were resolved, and it formed an important part of the legal order of medieval Europe.

At the bottom of the feudal social order were the peasants who worked the land, and many of these were serfs, whose legal status and obligations were an important part of the feudal system. Serfs were not free in the way that free peasants or the higher orders of society were free, and their status was one of the more difficult aspects of medieval society to reconcile with modern ideas about freedom and human dignity. A serf was bound to the land, meaning that the serf couldn't freely leave the land he worked but was tied to it, and if the land passed to a new lord, the serf passed with it. Serfs owed various obligations to the lord of the manor on which they lived, including labor services, working the lord's land for a certain number of days, and various dues and payments. In return, serfs had the use of land to support themselves and their families and were entitled to the protection of the lord and to remain on the land they worked.

The status of serfs was, however, distinct from slavery, and this distinction matters for understanding the medieval social order accurately. Serfs weren't the property of the lord in the way that slaves were property, and they had certain rights and protections, including the right to remain on their land and to pass it to their heirs, and a recognized place in the customary order of the manor. Serfs lived and worked according to the customs of the manor, which defined their obligations and their rights, and these customs provided a degree of protection and stability, even as they bound the serf to a subordinate position. The condition of serfdom was one of subordination and unfreedom, with serfs bound to the land and owing substantial obligations to their lords, but it was a status defined by mutual, if highly unequal, obligations and by the customs of the manor, rather than one of pure ownership and total lack of rights. Over the later medieval period, serfdom gradually declined in many parts of Western Europe, as economic and social changes led to the loosening and eventual disappearance of the ties that bound serfs to the land, though the pace and pattern of this change varied greatly across different regions.

The table below lays out the key relationships and obligations of the feudal order, showing how duties ran in both directions at each level.

Relationship	What the Superior Provided	What the Subordinate Owed
King and great lords	Grants of land, recognition of rights	Military service, loyalty, counsel, aids
Lord and vassal	A fief and its protection	Military service, loyalty, feudal dues
Lord of the manor and serf	Use of land, protection, a place on the manor	Labor services, dues, and payments

The Magna Carta (1215) and limits on royal power

In the year 1215, in a meadow called Runnymede beside the River Thames in England, a group of rebellious barons forced their king to affix his seal to a document that would become one of the most famous and influential legal documents in the history of the world. That document was Magna Carta, the "Great Charter," and though its immediate purpose was to resolve a specific political crisis of its own time, it came to stand for a principle of enormous and lasting importance: that the power of the ruler is not unlimited, and that even the king is subject to the law. The story of Magna Carta and of how it came to have this meaning is one of the most important in the history of law.

The immediate background to Magna Carta was a conflict between King John of England and his barons, the great lords of the kingdom. King John had made himself deeply unpopular through a combination of heavy taxation, arbitrary and abusive treatment of his barons, costly and unsuccessful wars, and conflicts with the Church. The barons, angered by the king's demands and his abuses of power, and by his disregard for their rights and the customs of the kingdom, rose in rebellion against him, and in 1215 they forced him to come to terms. The result of their negotiations was Magna Carta, a document in which the king agreed to a series of concessions and promises addressing the grievances of the barons and placing limits on his power.

Much of the actual content of Magna Carta concerned specific grievances of the barons and specific issues of the feudal law and politics of the time, and it's important to understand this to see the document accurately rather than through the lens of later interpretation alone. Many of its provisions dealt with particular feudal dues and obligations, with the king's treatment of the barons and their rights, and with various specific matters of concern to the barons in the circumstances of 1215. In its original context, Magna Carta was a practical document addressing the concrete grievances that had led to the rebellion, a peace treaty of sorts between the king and his barons, rather than a grand statement of abstract principles of liberty and the rule of law. Much of its detail is concerned with the specific feudal and political circumstances of early thirteenth-century England.

But Magna Carta also contained provisions of broader significance, provisions that expressed principles reaching well beyond the immediate circumstances of 1215, and it was these that gave the document its lasting importance and its enduring fame.

(King John was reluctant to sign the document because the Magna Carta would curb his power, especially over taxation, justice, and arbitrary rule. He viewed it as a forced concession to rebellious barons.)

Among the most important was a provision establishing that the king couldn't simply imprison, dispossess, or punish a free man arbitrarily, but only according to the lawful judgment of his equals or by the law of the land. This provision expressed a principle of profound importance: that even the king was bound by law in his treatment of his subjects and couldn't act against them arbitrarily and without legal process. It's often seen as an ancestor of the principle of due process of law, the idea that a person can't be deprived of life, liberty, or property except through proper legal procedures, and it stands as one of the most influential provisions in the history of law.

Another provision of lasting significance addressed the matter of justice, with the king promising that he wouldn't sell, deny, or delay justice to anyone. This expressed the principle that justice should be available to all and shouldn't be sold, denied, or delayed by the ruler, a principle of great importance for the development of ideas about access to justice and the proper administration of law. Provisions like these, expressing broad principles about the limits of royal power and the availability of justice, gave Magna Carta a significance that transcended the specific circumstances of its creation and made it a foundational document in the history of constitutional government and the rule of law.

The most important thing about Magna Carta, and the reason it became so famous and influential, was the principle it came to represent: that the power of the ruler is limited by law, and that even the king is subject to the law and can't rule arbitrarily and without regard to the rights of his subjects. This principle, that the ruler is not above the law but bound by it, is one of the most important ideas in the history of law and government, and it lies at the very foundation of constitutional government and the rule of law. Magna Carta, by placing the king under legal obligations and asserting that he couldn't act arbitrarily against his subjects, gave powerful expression to this principle, and over the centuries it came to stand as a great symbol of the idea that governmental power is limited by law and that even the highest authority must operate within legal bounds.

The later history of Magna Carta is a story of reinterpretation and of growing significance over time, and this is a crucial part of understanding its importance. In the centuries after 1215, Magna Carta was reissued and confirmed many times, and it gradually came to be regarded as a fundamental statement of English liberties and of the limits on royal power. In later periods, particularly in the seventeenth century during the great constitutional struggles between the English crown and Parliament, Magna Carta was invoked and reinterpreted as a foundational guarantee of English liberties and of the principle that the king was subject to the law. Later interpreters read into Magna Carta broad principles about liberty, the rule of law, and the limits on governmental power, principles that went well beyond what the document had originally meant in its thirteenth-century context. Through this process of reinterpretation, Magna Carta grew in significance and came to be seen as one of the great foundational documents of constitutional liberty, influencing the development of constitutional government not only in England but in other countries as well, including the development of constitutional ideas and documents in America.

The development of common law courts in England

While much of continental Europe was developing legal systems built on the revived foundation of Roman law, England took a different path, developing a distinctive legal system that would become known as the common law. The common law originated in medieval England, and it grew into one of the two great legal traditions of the modern world, the other being the civil law tradition of continental Europe descended from Roman law. The development of the common law in medieval England is therefore a matter of great importance for the history of law, because this English legal system would eventually spread across much of the world and shape the law of many nations.

The origins of the common law lie in the efforts of the medieval English kings, particularly following the Norman Conquest of England in 1066, to establish and extend royal justice throughout the kingdom. The Norman kings and their successors worked to build up a system of royal courts and royal justice that would apply throughout England, and the development of this royal justice was the foundation of the common law. A particularly important figure in this development was King Henry II, who reigned in the twelfth century and who did much to strengthen and extend the system of royal justice, introducing reforms that greatly advanced the development of the common law. Under Henry II and his successors, the system of royal courts and royal justice grew and developed, gradually establishing a body of law that applied throughout the kingdom.

The term common law itself reflects one of the essential features of this legal system, and understanding the name helps illuminate what made the system distinctive. The common law was called common because it was the law common to the whole of England, applying throughout the kingdom, as opposed to the various local and customary laws that had previously governed different parts of the country. The royal courts, in administering the king's justice throughout England, developed a body of law that was common to the entire kingdom, a single law applying everywhere rather than a patchwork of differing local customs. This unification of the law under a common system applying throughout the kingdom was one of the great achievements of the medieval English kings and one of the defining features of the common law.

A crucial and distinctive feature of the common law was the way it developed through the decisions of judges in actual cases.

The common law grew and developed as the royal judges decided the cases that came before them, and the decisions they made in these cases became precedents that guided the decision of later cases. Over time, the accumulated decisions of the judges built up a body of law, developed case by case as judges decided the disputes brought to them and as their decisions established principles that would be followed in future cases. This method of developing law through judicial decisions in actual cases, with past decisions serving as precedents for future ones, became the hallmark of the common law and distinguished it sharply from the civil law tradition of the continent, which developed more through comprehensive codes and the systematic legal science built on Roman law.

The principle that past judicial decisions should guide the decision of later cases came to be known by the Latin phrase stare decisis, meaning to stand by things decided, and it's fundamental to the common law tradition. Under this principle, when a court decides a case and establishes a legal principle in doing so, that principle becomes a precedent that should be followed in later cases involving similar circumstances. This gives the common law a particular character, one in which the law is found in the accumulated decisions of the courts and develops through the ongoing process of judicial decision-making, growing and adapting as new cases raise new questions and as courts apply and extend the principles established in earlier decisions. The reliance on precedent gives the common law both continuity, since courts follow the principles established in past cases, and a capacity to develop and adapt, since courts can extend and refine those principles as they apply them to new situations.

The common law was administered through a system of royal courts that developed over the medieval period, and these courts became the central institutions of the common law system. Several distinct royal courts emerged, each with its own particular areas of jurisdiction, and together they administered the king's justice and developed the common law through their decisions. The judges of these courts, in deciding the cases brought before them, developed and refined the principles of the common law, and the body of law they built up through their decisions became the foundation of the English legal system. The development of these royal courts and of the professional judges and lawyers who worked in them was an important part of the growth of the common law, establishing the institutional framework within which the common law developed and was administered.

The procedure of the common law had its own distinctive features, and one of these was of particular importance: the development of the jury. The use of juries, groups of ordinary people who decided questions of fact in legal cases, became an important feature of the common law system, and the jury came to occupy a significant place in the administration of justice under the common law. The jury system that developed in medieval England, in which questions of fact in both criminal and civil cases came to be decided by juries of ordinary people, became one of the distinctive and enduring features of the common law tradition, and it spread along with the common law to other countries, becoming an important institution in the legal systems of many nations that adopted the common law. The development of the jury as a means of deciding questions of fact was a significant contribution of the medieval English common law to the broader history of law.

Below we highlight the main differences between the two great legal traditions that took shape in medieval Europe and went on to govern much of the world.

Feature	**Common Law (England)**	**Civil Law (Continent)**
Primary source	Judicial decisions and precedent	Comprehensive codes based on Roman law
How law develops	Case by case through judges' rulings	Through systematic codes and legal science
Role of precedent	Central (stare decisis)	Less binding; codes are primary
Historical root	Royal justice of medieval England	Revived Roman law of Justinian
Use of the jury	Prominent and enduring	Historically less central

The development of the common law in medieval England had consequences that extended far beyond England itself, and this is what makes it so significant for the broader history of law. The common law became the foundation of the English legal system, and as England's influence spread across the world in later centuries, the common law spread with it, becoming the basis of the legal systems of many nations. The common law tradition, with its reliance on judicial decisions and precedent, its distinctive courts and procedures, and its characteristic institutions such as the jury, took root in many parts of the world that came under English influence, and it became one of the two great legal traditions of the modern world. Today, the common law tradition governs the law of England and of many nations whose legal systems descend from the English common law, standing alongside the civil law tradition of continental Europe as one of the two principal families of legal systems in the world. The medieval English common law, developed by the royal judges of medieval England deciding the cases brought before them, thus became one of the great foundations of law across the modern world, a legacy of the medieval English legal system that endures to this day.

Discussion question: Medieval Europe had no single legal authority but instead many overlapping systems, canon law, feudal law, royal law, town law, and merchant law, all operating at once and often competing with one another. We tend to assume that a unified legal system with one clear source of authority is better, yet this messy medieval competition among rival legal orders may have helped produce the very ideas about limited power and the rule of law that we most value. Could the absence of a single dominant legal authority have been a strength rather than a weakness, and if so, what does that suggest about whether concentrating all legal authority in one place is truly desirable?

Chapter 7: Islamic Law and Its Development

In the seventh century, in the arid lands of the Arabian Peninsula, a new religion arose that would transform much of the world, and with it came a new and comprehensive system of law. Islam brought not only a faith but a complete framework for living, one in which law occupied a central place, because Islam understood law as the expression of God's will for how human beings should conduct their lives. This system of Islamic law, developed over the centuries following the birth of Islam, became one of the great legal traditions of human history, governing the lives of hundreds of millions of people across a vast region stretching from Spain to Southeast Asia, and it remains a living and influential legal tradition today, shaping the lives of well over a billion Muslims around the world.

Islamic law differs in important ways from the legal traditions we've examined so far, and understanding these differences is essential to understanding Islamic law on its own terms. Where Roman law was fundamentally a human legal science developed by jurists reasoning about practical problems, and where the common law developed through the decisions of judges in cases, Islamic law is understood by Muslims as being rooted in divine revelation, in God's guidance for humanity as revealed through the Prophet Muhammad.

This gives Islamic law a distinctive character, as a system understood to derive its authority ultimately from God rather than from human legislators or judges, and as a system that encompasses not only what we might think of as law in the narrow sense but a comprehensive guide to right conduct in all areas of life, religious and worldly alike.

The scope of Islamic law is broad, extending far beyond the matters that a modern secular legal system would address, and this breadth reflects the Islamic understanding of law as guidance for the whole of life. Islamic law addresses not only matters like contracts, property, marriage, inheritance, and crime, which we'd recognize as legal subjects, but also matters of religious worship and ritual, personal conduct and ethics, and the relationship between the believer and God. In the Islamic understanding, all of these fall within the scope of God's guidance for humanity, and Islamic law therefore encompasses the whole range of human conduct, providing guidance on how a Muslim should live in accordance with God's will in every aspect of life. This comprehensive scope is one of the distinctive features of Islamic law and reflects the Islamic vision of a life lived wholly in accordance with divine guidance.

The Quran and Hadith as sources of legal authority

The foundation of Islamic law rests on its sources, the authoritative bases from which the law is derived, and understanding these sources is the essential starting point for understanding Islamic law as a whole. Islamic law is derived from several sources, arranged in a hierarchy of authority, and the two most important and authoritative of these are the Quran and the Hadith, which together form the primary foundation of Islamic law. From these sources, along with other methods of legal reasoning, the vast body of Islamic law was developed over the centuries by generations of Muslim legal scholars.

The Quran is the holy book of Islam, understood by Muslims to be the word of God as revealed to the Prophet Muhammad, and it stands as the highest and most authoritative source of Islamic law. As the revealed word of God, the Quran is the ultimate foundation of Islamic law, and its provisions carry the highest authority.

The Quran contains guidance on many matters, including matters of law, and among its verses are a number that address legal subjects directly, providing rules on matters such as marriage, divorce, inheritance, contracts, and various other legal questions, as well as on matters of crime and punishment. These legal verses of the Quran provide the foundational legal material from which important parts of Islamic law are derived, and they carry the supreme authority that belongs to the revealed word of God.

It's worth understanding, however, that while the Quran is the highest source of Islamic law, only a portion of its content deals directly with legal matters in the narrow sense, and much of the detailed law of Islam had to be developed from the foundation the Quran provides through further sources and methods of reasoning. The Quran provides essential legal guidance and foundational principles, but it isn't a comprehensive legal code addressing every legal question in detail. Much of the Quran addresses matters of faith, worship, morality, and the relationship between people and God, and its legal provisions, while of the highest authority, don't by themselves constitute a complete and detailed system of law covering every situation. The development of a comprehensive body of Islamic law therefore required drawing on additional sources and methods beyond the Quran itself, building on the foundation the Quran provided.

The second great source of Islamic law is the Hadith, and understanding the Hadith and its role is essential to understanding how Islamic law developed. The Hadith are the recorded traditions concerning the sayings, actions, and approvals of the Prophet Muhammad, the accounts of what the Prophet said and did and of what he approved or permitted. Because the Prophet Muhammad is regarded in Islam as the model of proper conduct and as the person who best understood and exemplified God's guidance, his example, known as the Sunnah and recorded in the Hadith, became a source of law of great authority, second only to the Quran itself. The Hadith provide guidance on many matters not addressed in detail in the Quran, and they became an essential source for the development of Islamic law, supplementing and elaborating the guidance of the Quran.

The Hadith developed into an enormous body of material, as the traditions concerning the Prophet were collected, recorded, and transmitted over the generations following his death, and this raised an important question that became central to the development of Islamic law: how to determine which of the many reported traditions were authentic and reliable. Because the Hadith were transmitted orally at first and then collected and written down over time, and because their

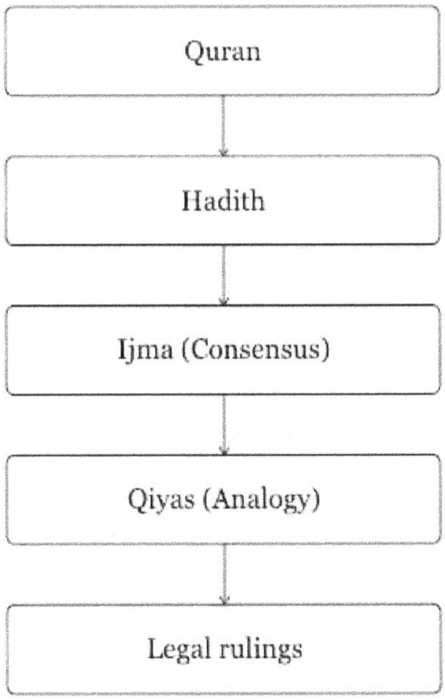

authority as a source of law depended on their being genuine accounts of what the Prophet actually said and did, Muslim scholars developed methods for evaluating the authenticity and reliability of the reported traditions. They examined the chains of transmission by which each tradition had been passed down, tracing the reported tradition back through the successive people who had transmitted it to determine whether the chain of transmission was reliable and whether the tradition could be considered authentic. Through this careful process of evaluation, scholars sought to distinguish authentic and reliable traditions from those that were weak, doubtful, or fabricated, and they produced great collections of Hadith that gathered together the traditions considered most reliable. This work of collecting and evaluating the Hadith was a major scholarly achievement and an essential part of establishing the foundation of Islamic law.

Beyond the Quran and the Hadith, Islamic legal scholars developed additional sources and methods for deriving law, and these became important elements in the development of the comprehensive body of Islamic law. Two of these deserve particular mention because of their importance in Islamic legal reasoning. One is consensus, known as ijma, which refers to the agreement of the scholars, or of the community, on a point of law. Where the qualified scholars reached agreement on a legal question, this consensus came to be regarded as a source of authority, on the reasoning that the community or its scholars, taken as a whole, would not agree on an error. The other is analogical reasoning, known as qiyas, which refers to the method of extending the law to new situations by reasoning from the established rules by analogy. Where a new situation arose that wasn't directly addressed in the Quran or the Hadith, scholars could reason by analogy from an established rule addressing a similar situation, extending the underlying principle to cover the new case. Through these methods, along with the primary sources of the Quran and the Hadith, Islamic scholars developed the comprehensive body of Islamic law, deriving detailed legal rules covering the wide range of matters within the scope of Islamic law.

The principal sources of Islamic law in their order of authority, along with what each contributes.

Source	Arabic Term	Nature	Authority
The Quran	Qur'an	The revealed word of God	Highest and foundational
The example of the Prophet	Sunnah/ Hadith	Sayings and actions of Muhammad	Second only to the Quran
Consensus of scholars	Ijma	Agreement on a point of law	A recognized source
Analogical reasoning	Qiyas	Extending rules to new cases by analogy	A recognized method

The relationship among these sources, and the methods by which they were used to derive law, became the subject of a sophisticated science of Islamic jurisprudence, and this points toward the broader intellectual achievement of Islamic legal scholarship. The study of the sources of law and of the proper methods for deriving legal rules from them developed into a refined discipline, the science of the roots or foundations of the law, which examined the sources of Islamic law and the principles and methods of legal reasoning. This science provided the theoretical foundation for the work of deriving the detailed rules of Islamic law from the authoritative sources, and it represents a significant intellectual achievement, a sophisticated theory of the sources of law and of legal reasoning developed by Muslim scholars over the centuries. The development of this jurisprudence, alongside the derivation of the detailed rules of law themselves, made Islamic legal scholarship one of the great achievements of Islamic civilization and one of the sophisticated legal sciences in the history of law.

The four major schools of Sunni jurisprudence

As Islamic law developed over the centuries following the birth of Islam, different schools of legal thought emerged, each with its own approach to the derivation and interpretation of the law, and these schools became a defining feature of the Islamic legal tradition. In Sunni Islam, the largest branch of Islam, four major schools of jurisprudence came to be recognized, and these four schools have shaped Sunni Islamic law down to the present day.

Understanding these schools and their role is important for understanding the character of Islamic law, which developed not as a single uniform system but as a tradition encompassing different schools of thought that shared a common foundation while differing in various matters of legal interpretation and detail.

The emergence of different schools of Islamic legal thought reflected the fact that the derivation of law from the sources involved interpretation and reasoning, and that scholars could differ in their approaches and conclusions. Because the development of Islamic law required interpreting the sources and reasoning from them to derive detailed legal rules, and because this process left room for differences of interpretation and method, different scholars and different centers of legal scholarship developed somewhat different approaches to the law.

Over time, these differences crystallized into distinct schools of jurisprudence, each associated with a founding scholar or scholars and each developing its own body of legal doctrine and its own characteristic approaches to the interpretation of the law. These schools weren't rival religions or fundamentally opposed systems, but different approaches within the shared framework of Sunni Islamic law, agreeing on the fundamentals while differing on various matters of interpretation and detail.

The four major Sunni schools each came to be associated with a founding scholar after whom the school was named, and each developed a distinctive approach and body of doctrine. The Hanafi school is associated with the scholar Abu Hanifa and became known for an approach that gave significant scope to reasoning in the derivation of law. The Maliki school is associated with the scholar Malik ibn Anas and gave particular weight to the practice of the community of Medina, the city where the Prophet had established the early Muslim community, as a source of legal authority. The Shafi'i school is associated with the scholar al-Shafi'i, who made important contributions to the theory of the sources of Islamic law and to the systematic understanding of how law should be derived from the sources. The Hanbali school is associated with the scholar Ahmad ibn Hanbal and became known for an approach that emphasized close adherence to the Quran and the Hadith. Each of these four schools developed its own body of legal doctrine and its own characteristic methods, and each gained followings in different regions of the Muslim world.

The four schools came to predominate in different geographic regions of the Muslim world, and this geographic distribution of the schools became a lasting feature of the Islamic legal landscape. Different regions came to follow different schools, so that a particular school might predominate in one part of the Muslim world while another school predominated elsewhere.

This meant that while all four schools were recognized as legitimate within Sunni Islam, the law as actually applied in a given region reflected the school that predominated there, giving rise to regional variations in Islamic law corresponding to the different schools followed in different areas. This distribution of the schools across different regions contributed to a degree of variation in Islamic law from place to place, even as all the schools shared the common foundation of Sunni Islamic jurisprudence.

An important feature of the relationship among the four schools was the mutual recognition of their legitimacy, and this mutual recognition is significant for understanding the character of the Islamic legal tradition. The four schools recognized one another as legitimate and valid approaches to Islamic law, accepting that differences among them on matters of interpretation and detail were acceptable variations within the shared framework of Sunni Islamic law rather than fundamental errors or departures from the faith. This mutual recognition reflected an acceptance of a degree of legitimate diversity in the interpretation of the law, an acknowledgment that qualified scholars might reasonably reach different conclusions on various legal questions and that these differences were an acceptable feature of the legal tradition. This acceptance of legitimate diversity within a shared framework was a notable feature of Sunni Islamic law, allowing for variation and difference among the schools while maintaining the underlying unity of the tradition.

The development of the four schools and their bodies of doctrine represented a great achievement of Islamic legal scholarship, producing an enormous body of legal learning developed over the centuries by the scholars of the various schools. Each school developed a substantial literature, including works expounding its legal doctrine, works on the theory of the sources and methods of the law, and works applying the law to the many detailed questions that arose. This vast body of legal scholarship, produced by generations of scholars across the four schools, constitutes one of the great intellectual achievements of Islamic civilization, a sophisticated and comprehensive body of legal learning covering the wide range of matters within the scope of Islamic law. The four schools and their scholarship gave Sunni Islamic law its characteristic form, as a tradition of legal learning encompassing different schools of thought that shared a common foundation while developing their own distinctive doctrines and approaches.

It should be noted that the branch of Islam known as Shia Islam developed its own tradition of jurisprudence, distinct from the Sunni schools, and this is worth mentioning for a complete picture of the Islamic legal tradition. Shia Islam, the second major branch of Islam, has its own school or schools of legal thought, with their own approaches to the derivation and interpretation of Islamic law, reflecting the distinct religious traditions and authorities of Shia Islam. While this chapter focuses primarily on the four major schools of Sunni jurisprudence, which govern the law for the majority of Muslims, the Shia tradition of jurisprudence is an important part of the broader Islamic legal tradition, and it developed its own sophisticated body of legal learning. The existence of both the Sunni schools and the Shia tradition reflects the diversity within the broader Islamic legal tradition, which encompasses different branches and schools while sharing the common foundation of the Quran and the fundamental sources of Islamic law.

Sharia in commercial, family, and criminal law

Islamic law, often referred to as Sharia, addresses a wide range of subjects, and examining how it deals with several major areas of law helps to convey the character and substance of the Islamic legal tradition.

The term Sharia refers to the divine law of Islam, God's guidance for how human beings should live, and it encompasses the comprehensive body of Islamic law covering the wide range of matters within its scope. Looking at how Islamic law addresses commercial matters, family matters, and criminal matters gives a sense of the substance of Islamic law and of how it regulates important areas of human life, though these are only some of the many areas that Islamic law addresses.

In the area of commercial and financial law, Islamic law developed a sophisticated body of rules governing trade, business, contracts, and financial transactions, reflecting the importance of commerce in the Islamic world and the concern of Islamic law with regulating economic life in accordance with its principles. Islamic commercial law addressed the formation and performance of contracts, the conduct of trade and business, partnerships and other business arrangements, and a wide range of commercial and financial matters. A distinctive and important feature of Islamic commercial law was its prohibition of certain practices considered unjust or exploitative, and the most notable of these was the prohibition of riba, which is often understood as the prohibition of interest or usury.

The prohibition of riba is one of the most distinctive features of Islamic commercial and financial law, and it has significant implications for how financial transactions are conducted in accordance with Islamic law. Riba, commonly understood as the charging of interest on loans, is prohibited in Islamic law, on the basis that it involves an unjust gain, the making of money from money without genuine productive activity or the sharing of real risk. This prohibition meant that the ordinary lending of money at interest, which is central to conventional finance, was not permitted under Islamic law, and it led to the development of alternative financial arrangements and structures designed to enable financial and commercial activity while avoiding prohibited interest. Islamic law developed various forms of permissible financial arrangements, such as arrangements based on the sharing of profit and loss, or on trade and the buying and selling of goods, that allowed for financing and investment while conforming to the prohibition of riba. This concern with avoiding interest and with structuring financial transactions in accordance with Islamic principles has continued into the modern era, giving rise to the field of modern Islamic finance and banking, which seeks to provide financial services in accordance with Islamic law, including its prohibition of interest.

Islamic law also placed importance on fairness and the avoidance of excessive uncertainty and exploitation in commercial dealings, reflecting a broader concern with justice in economic relationships. In addition to the prohibition of interest, Islamic commercial law addressed other practices considered problematic, including excessive uncertainty or ambiguity in contracts and various forms of exploitation or unfairness in dealings. This reflected a concern that commercial and financial dealings should be conducted fairly and honestly, without exploitation, excessive uncertainty, or unjust gain, and it gave Islamic commercial law a distinctive ethical dimension, concerned not only with the technical rules governing transactions but with ensuring that economic dealings conformed to principles of fairness and justice. This ethical concern with fairness in commercial dealings is an important feature of Islamic commercial law and reflects the broader Islamic understanding of law as guidance for living rightly in accordance with God's will.

In the area of family law, Islamic law developed a detailed body of rules governing marriage, divorce, and family relationships, and family law has been one of the most important and enduring areas of Islamic law. Islamic family law addressed the formation of marriage, the rights and obligations of spouses, the dissolution of marriage through divorce, the custody and care of children, and related matters, providing a comprehensive framework for the regulation of family life. Marriage in

Islamic law is understood as a contract, with rights and obligations on both sides, and Islamic law set out detailed rules governing the marriage contract, the obligations of the husband and wife to one another, and the various matters concerning the marital relationship. Islamic family law also addressed divorce, providing for the dissolution of marriage under various circumstances and setting out the rules and procedures governing divorce and its consequences.

Inheritance is another important area addressed by Islamic law, and Islamic inheritance law is notable for its detail and for the specific shares it prescribes for various heirs. Islamic law developed detailed rules governing the inheritance of property after death, specifying the shares of the estate that various heirs were entitled to receive. The Quran itself contains provisions on inheritance, specifying shares for various relatives, and Islamic inheritance law developed these provisions into a detailed system prescribing how an estate should be divided among the heirs. This system of inheritance, with its specific prescribed shares for various heirs, is a distinctive and detailed part of Islamic law, and it governs the distribution of property after death in accordance with the rules laid down in the sources of Islamic law. The detail and specificity of Islamic inheritance law reflect the importance attached to the proper distribution of property among heirs and the concern of Islamic law with regulating this important matter in accordance with divine guidance.

In the area of criminal law, Islamic law addressed offenses and their punishments, and this is an area that has attracted particular attention, including in discussions of Islamic law in the modern world. Islamic criminal law addressed various offenses, and it included a category of specific offenses for which particular punishments were prescribed in the sources of Islamic law. These offenses, for which fixed punishments were specified, were regarded as offenses against the limits set by God, and the punishments prescribed for them were understood to derive from the authoritative sources of Islamic law. Islamic criminal law also included other categories of offenses, including offenses for which the punishment was left to the discretion of the judge, and matters of retaliation and compensation for offenses against persons, such as injury and homicide, which drew on the ancient principles of retaliation and compensation that we've encountered in other legal traditions. The application of Islamic criminal law, and particularly of the specific prescribed punishments, has been a significant matter in the modern world, where different countries and communities have taken different approaches to the application of Islamic criminal law, and where the prescribed punishments have been the subject of considerable discussion and debate.

The role of the qadi in adjudicating disputes

The administration of Islamic law required institutions and officials to apply the law and resolve disputes, and the central figure in the administration of Islamic law was the qadi, the Islamic judge. The qadi occupied an important position in the Islamic legal system, being the official responsible for hearing cases, applying Islamic law, and rendering judgments in the disputes brought before him, and understanding the role of the qadi is important for understanding how Islamic law functioned in practice. The qadi was the judge who administered Islamic law in the courts, applying the law developed by the scholars to the actual cases and disputes that arose in the community.

The qadi was appointed to his position by the ruler or by an appropriate authority, and he exercised judicial authority in the name of that authority, hearing cases and rendering judgments in accordance with Islamic law. The qadi's function was to apply Islamic law to the cases brought before him, determining the facts of each case and applying the relevant rules of Islamic law to reach a judgment. In performing this function, the qadi drew on the body of Islamic law developed by the scholars, applying the rules and principles of the law, as developed within the relevant school of jurisprudence, to the particular circumstances of each case. **The qadi thus served as the point at which the body of Islamic law, developed through the scholarship of the jurists, was applied to actual disputes and given practical effect in the resolution of the conflicts that arose in the community**.

An important aspect of the qadi's role was the relationship between the judge and the scholars of the law, and this relationship reflects a distinctive feature of the Islamic legal system. While the qadi was the official who applied the law and rendered judgments, the law itself was developed primarily by the scholars, the jurists who studied the sources, reasoned about the law, and developed the detailed rules and doctrines of Islamic law within the various schools. There was, in effect, a distinction between the development of the law, which was the work of the scholars, and the application of the law, which was the function of the qadi. In deciding difficult questions, a qadi might seek the opinion of a qualified scholar, a mufti, who could give an authoritative opinion, known as a fatwa, on a point of law. This meant that the qadi, in applying the law, could draw on the learning of the scholars, and that the application of the law by the judge was connected to the ongoing scholarly development and interpretation of the law by the jurists. This relationship between the judge who applied the law and the scholars who developed and interpreted it was a characteristic feature of the Islamic legal system.

The procedure followed by the qadi in hearing cases had its own features, drawing on the principles of Islamic law concerning the conduct of legal proceedings and the determination of the facts. The qadi heard the cases brought before him, considered the evidence presented, and reached a judgment based on his determination of the facts and his application of the relevant law.

Islamic law had rules concerning evidence and proof, including rules about the testimony of witnesses and the taking of oaths, and the qadi applied these rules in determining the facts of the cases before him. The qadi's determination of the facts, based on the evidence presented in accordance with the rules of Islamic law, together with his application of the relevant legal rules, formed the basis of his judgment in each case. The procedure of the qadi's court thus combined the determination of the facts, according to the rules of evidence and proof, with the application of the substantive law, to reach a resolution of the dispute.

The office of the qadi and the courts over which the qadi presided were important institutions in the societies governed by Islamic law, providing the means by which disputes were resolved and justice administered in accordance with the law. Throughout the lands of the Muslim world, qadis administered Islamic law in the courts, resolving the disputes and controversies that arose in the community and giving practical effect to the body of Islamic law. The administration of justice by the qadis was an essential function in these societies, maintaining order, resolving conflicts, and applying the law to the affairs of the community, and the office of the qadi was accordingly an important and respected position. Through the work of the qadis in the courts, the body of Islamic law developed by the scholars was applied to the actual affairs of the community, and justice was administered in accordance with the law, making the qadi a central figure in the practical functioning of the Islamic legal system.

Islamic law's influence on medieval trade and contract

Islamic law, and particularly Islamic commercial law, had an influence that extended beyond the Muslim world itself, and this influence on medieval trade and commerce is an important part of the broader significance of Islamic law in the history of law. During the medieval period, the Muslim world was a center of trade and commerce, connected through extensive trade networks that linked the lands of the Muslim world with one another and with regions beyond, including Europe. In this context of active and far-reaching commerce, Islamic commercial law developed sophisticated instruments and practices for the conduct of trade and business, and some of these had an influence that reached beyond the Muslim world, contributing to the development of commercial practices and instruments in medieval Europe and beyond.

The medieval Muslim world was, for much of the medieval period, a region of flourishing trade, commerce, and economic activity, connected by trade routes that carried goods across vast distances, from within the Muslim lands to regions far beyond. This active commerce created a need for sophisticated commercial and financial instruments and practices, means of facilitating trade, providing financing, transferring value over distances, and organizing business ventures, and Islamic commercial law developed a range of such instruments and practices to meet these needs. Islamic commercial law provided the legal framework for this flourishing commerce, developing the contracts, partnerships, and other arrangements that enabled trade and business to be conducted, and doing so in a manner that conformed to the principles of Islamic law, including its prohibition of interest and its concern with fairness in dealings.

Among the instruments and practices developed in connection with medieval Muslim commerce were various forms of business partnership and financial arrangement, and these arrangements enabled the organization of trade and the provision of financing in ways consistent with Islamic law. Islamic commercial law developed forms of partnership in which parties could combine capital and effort in a business venture and share in the resulting profits, providing means of organizing trade and business and of providing financing for commercial ventures.

One important form of arrangement allowed one party to provide capital and another to provide the effort and labor of conducting the trade or venture, with the profits shared between them according to agreement, providing a means of financing trade that conformed to Islamic law by involving the sharing of profit and risk rather than the charging of interest. Arrangements of this kind enabled the provision of financing and the organization of commercial ventures in a manner consistent with Islamic principles, and they were important instruments in the conduct of medieval Muslim commerce.

Islamic commerce also made use of various instruments for the transfer of value and the facilitation of trade over distances, and these instruments were significant for the conduct of long-distance commerce. In a world of extensive trade over long distances, means of transferring value and of facilitating payment and credit across distances were important, and Islamic commercial practice developed instruments that could serve these functions. Such instruments could enable the transfer of value or the provision of credit across distances, facilitating trade by reducing the need to transport large quantities of coin or goods and by providing means of payment and credit that could operate across the extensive trade networks of the medieval world. Instruments of this kind were valuable in the conduct of long-distance trade, and they contributed to the sophistication and reach of medieval Muslim commerce.

The influence of these Islamic commercial instruments and practices on medieval Europe is a matter of significance for the history of commercial law, and it reflects the broader connections between the Muslim world and Europe during the medieval period. Through the extensive contacts between the Muslim world and Europe, including trade, the interaction in regions where Muslim and European commerce met, and other channels of contact and exchange, commercial practices and instruments developed in the Muslim world could become known in Europe and could influence the development of European commercial practice. Some of the commercial instruments and practices that developed in medieval Europe show similarities to instruments and practices found in the Muslim world, and it's thought that the sophisticated commercial practices of the Muslim world influenced the development of commercial practices in medieval Europe, contributing to the development of European commercial instruments and to the growth of European commerce. In this way, Islamic commercial law and practice had an influence that extended beyond the Muslim world, contributing to the broader development of commercial law and practice, including in Europe.

Outlining several features of Islamic commercial law and their significance for medieval trade.

Feature	**Nature**	**Significance**
Prohibition of riba	Ban on interest and unjust gain	Led to profit-and-loss sharing arrangements
Partnership arrangements	Combining capital and labor with shared profit	Enabled financing of trade without interest
Instruments of transfer and credit	Means of moving value across distances	Facilitated long-distance commerce
Concern with fairness	Avoidance of excessive uncertainty and exploitation	Gave commercial dealings an ethical dimension

The significance of Islamic law in the history of law extends well beyond its influence on medieval commerce, important as that was, and it's worth recognizing the broader importance of Islamic law as one of the great legal traditions of human history. Islamic law governed the lives of vast populations across a great expanse of the world over many centuries, providing a comprehensive framework of law and guidance for living that shaped the societies of the Muslim world. It represents a sophisticated and highly developed legal tradition, the product of centuries of scholarship and legal reasoning by generations of Muslim scholars who developed the comprehensive body of Islamic law from its foundational sources. And it remains a living and influential legal tradition today, continuing to shape the lives of well over a billion Muslims around the world and continuing to develop as it addresses the circumstances of the modern world.

As one of the major legal traditions of human history, comparable in its scope, sophistication, and influence to the other great legal traditions we've examined, Islamic law occupies an important place in the history of law, and understanding it is essential to understanding the full range of the ways that human societies have developed law to govern their affairs and to pursue justice in accordance with their deepest values and beliefs.

Discussion question: Islamic law is understood by Muslims to derive its authority from divine revelation, yet in practice it was developed over centuries through human scholarship, interpretation, analogical reasoning, and the acceptance of legitimate differences among schools. How can a legal system hold together the belief that its foundation is unchanging divine law with the reality that human beings must constantly interpret, reason about, and apply that law to ever-changing circumstances, and does this tension between the divine and the human weaken such a system or give it a particular kind of strength that purely human-made legal systems might lack?

Chapter 8: The Rise of Common Law and Equity

The English common law didn't spring into existence fully formed. It grew over centuries, shaped by the ambitions of kings, the work of judges, the demands of ordinary people seeking justice, and the gradual accumulation of decisions and precedents that built up into a coherent body of law. In tracing this growth, we encounter some of the most important developments in the history of law, developments that gave the common law its distinctive character and that produced institutions and principles still central to the legal systems of much of the world today. This chapter follows the rise of the common law and the emergence alongside it of a second body of law, equity, which arose to address the shortcomings of the common law and became an essential part of the English legal tradition.

The story we'll follow has several threads. There's the strengthening of royal justice under the medieval English kings, which laid the foundation of the common law and gave England a unified legal system applying throughout the kingdom. There's the development of the doctrine of precedent, the principle that past decisions guide future ones, which became the defining method of the common law and shaped how the law developed and how judges did their work. There's the rise of equity, a body of law that grew up to soften the rigidity of the common law and to provide justice where the ordinary law fell short. And there's the beginning of legislation by Parliament, the making of law by statute, which introduced a new source of law alongside the judge-made common law and would grow over time into the dominant source of law in the modern age. Together, these developments shaped the English legal system and, through it, the legal systems of the many nations that inherited the English legal tradition.

Henry II's court reforms and the emergence of common law

Among the medieval English kings who contributed to the development of the common law, one stands out for the importance of his contribution: Henry II, who reigned in the twelfth century.

Henry II did more than perhaps any other single ruler to establish and strengthen the system of royal justice that became the foundation of the common law, and his reforms mark a crucial stage in the emergence of the common law as a unified system of law applying throughout England. Understanding Henry II's reforms is essential to understanding the origins of the common law, because it was through the strengthening of royal justice under Henry II and his successors that the common law took shape.

When Henry II came to the throne, England had a variety of courts and a variety of laws, including local courts administering local customs, the courts of the feudal lords, and the courts of the Church, alongside the justice of the king. Henry II worked to strengthen and extend royal justice, building up the system of royal courts and expanding the reach of the king's justice throughout the kingdom. He did this in part because strengthening royal justice strengthened royal power and authority, extending the king's reach into the administration of justice throughout the realm, and in part because a stronger and more effective system of royal justice served the interests of order and of the many people who sought justice. Through his reforms, Henry II greatly expanded the role of royal justice and laid the foundation for the common law as a unified system applying throughout England.

One of Henry II's most important innovations was the use of traveling royal judges, and this innovation was central to the development of a common law applying throughout the kingdom.

Henry II sent royal judges out from the central royal court to travel throughout the country, hearing cases in the various regions of the kingdom and bringing the king's justice to the localities. These traveling judges, going out on circuits through the country, heard cases throughout the realm and applied the king's justice everywhere they went, and this had a profound effect on the development of the law.

Because the same royal judges, applying the same royal justice, traveled throughout the kingdom hearing cases in different regions, the law they applied became common to the whole kingdom, a single body of law applying everywhere rather than a patchwork of differing local customs. The traveling royal judges thus became instruments for the development and spread of a common law throughout England, unifying the law of the kingdom under the king's justice.

Henry II also introduced important reforms in legal procedure that expanded the reach and effectiveness of royal justice, and these procedural innovations were significant for the development of the common law. He developed the use of the writ, a formal written order that could be obtained from the royal authority to initiate a legal action in the royal courts, and the writ system became central to the operation of the common law. A person seeking justice in the royal courts would obtain the appropriate writ, which set the legal action in motion, and the various writs corresponded to various kinds of legal claims and actions. Henry II also advanced the use of juries, groups of local people who could be called upon to determine questions of fact, including in disputes over land and other matters, and the development of the jury became an important feature of the common law. Through these procedural reforms, Henry II expanded the means by which people could seek and obtain royal justice, and he shaped the procedures through which the common law would operate.

The effect of Henry II's reforms was to establish royal justice as a strong and attractive system that drew cases to the royal courts and expanded the reach of the common law, and this had lasting consequences for the English legal system. As royal justice became stronger, more effective, and more available, people increasingly brought their disputes to the royal courts, and the royal courts and the common law they administered grew in importance relative to the older local courts, feudal courts, and other jurisdictions. The common law administered by the royal courts became the principal law of the land, applying throughout the kingdom and drawing to itself the resolution of an increasing range of disputes. Henry II's reforms thus set the common law on the path to becoming the dominant legal system of England, and they established the foundation of royal courts, royal judges, and royal justice on which the common law would develop over the following centuries. The strengthening of royal justice under Henry II was, in this sense, the crucial foundation of the common law, and Henry II deserves recognition as one of the most important figures in the origins of the common law tradition.

Precedent, stare decisis, and the role of judges

The common law is often described as judge-made law, and this description captures something essential about the nature of the common law and about how it developed. Unlike a legal system based primarily on comprehensive written codes, the common law developed principally through the decisions of judges in actual cases, with the accumulated decisions of the courts building up over time into the body of the common law. The mechanism by which this happened, the principle that past decisions guide the decision of future cases, is fundamental to the common law tradition, and understanding it is essential to understanding what makes the common law distinctive as a way of developing and applying law.

The central principle here is that of precedent, the idea that when a court decides a case and establishes a legal principle in doing so, that decision serves as a precedent that should guide the decision of later cases involving similar circumstances. Under this principle, the law is found in the decisions of the courts, and it develops as courts decide new cases, establish new principles, and apply and extend the principles established in earlier decisions.

This gives the common law a particular character, one in which the law grows organically through the ongoing process of judicial decision-making, developing case by case as courts confront new situations and as the accumulated body of decisions grows and is refined over time. The reliance on precedent means that the common law is always developing through the decisions of the courts, growing and adapting as new cases raise new questions.

The formal principle governing the use of precedent is known by the Latin phrase stare decisis, meaning to stand by things decided, and this principle is at the heart of the common law method. Under the principle of stare decisis, courts should follow the precedents established in earlier decisions, deciding like cases in like manner and adhering to the principles established in past decisions when deciding similar cases. This principle gives the common law both stability and predictability, because it means that the law established in past decisions will be followed in future cases, allowing people to know the law and to rely on it, and ensuring that similar cases are decided similarly rather than according to the differing views of different judges.

At the same time, the common law retains a capacity to develop and adapt, because courts can extend and refine the principles established in earlier decisions as they apply them to new situations, and because higher courts can, in appropriate circumstances, depart from or overrule earlier decisions that are found to be mistaken or no longer suitable. The principle of stare decisis thus balances the need for stability and predictability in the law with the capacity for the law to develop and adapt over time.

The role of judges in the common law system is distinctive, and it reflects the character of the common law as judge-made law developed through judicial decisions. In the common law tradition, judges don't merely apply the law but, in an important sense, develop and shape it through their decisions, establishing the principles that become precedents and that form the body of the common law. When a common law judge decides a case, particularly a case raising a new question or an unclear point of law, the judge's decision contributes to the development of the law, establishing or refining a principle that will guide future cases. This gives common law judges a significant role in the development of the law, a role that distinguishes the common law tradition from legal traditions in which the making of law is primarily the function of legislators and the role of judges is more strictly confined to applying the law that legislators have made. The distinctive role of the judge in developing the law through decisions is a characteristic feature of the common law tradition.

An important aspect of the common law method is the way that judges reason from precedents in deciding cases, and this reasoning is central to how the common law operates in practice. In deciding a case, a common law judge considers the relevant precedents, the earlier decisions bearing on the question at hand, and reasons about how those precedents apply to the case before the court. This involves determining what principle the earlier decisions established, considering whether and how that principle applies to the present case, and reasoning about the similarities and differences between the present case and the earlier ones. Where the facts of the present case are similar to those of an earlier case, the principle established in the earlier case may govern the present one; where the facts differ in ways that matter, the judge may distinguish the present case from the earlier one and reach a different result. This process of reasoning from precedents, comparing cases, and determining how the principles established in earlier decisions apply to new situations is the characteristic mode of legal reasoning in the common law tradition, and it's through this reasoning that the common law is applied and developed in the deciding of cases.

The common law method of developing law through precedent has both strengths and limitations, and recognizing both gives a balanced understanding of this distinctive approach to law. Among its strengths is its capacity to develop gradually and organically in response to actual cases and real situations, allowing the law to grow and adapt as new circumstances arise and as the courts confront new questions, while maintaining continuity with the principles established in past decisions. The common law can be responsive to the particular circumstances of cases and can develop nuanced principles refined through their application to many different situations over time. Among its limitations is that the development of law through the accumulation of case decisions can produce a body of law that's complex and sometimes difficult to determine, requiring the study of many decisions to ascertain the applicable principles, and the dependence on the cases that happen to come before the courts means that the development of the law is shaped by the accidents of litigation. Despite these limitations, the common law method of developing law through precedent has proven to be an effective and enduring approach to law, and it remains the characteristic method of the common law tradition, which governs the law of many nations around the world.

Courts of Chancery and the origins of equity

As the common law developed, it became more established, more fixed, and in some ways more rigid, and this rigidity gave rise to a problem that led to one of the most important developments in the history of English law: the emergence of equity. The common law, for all its strengths, could sometimes produce results that were unfair or inadequate, failing to provide justice in particular cases because of its rigidity, its technical requirements, or the limitations of the remedies it offered. To address this problem, a separate body of law, equity, grew up alongside the common law, administered through a distinct court, and equity became an essential part of the English legal tradition, providing justice where the common law fell short.

The problem that gave rise to equity was that the common law, as it became more fixed and established, could fail to provide adequate justice in certain cases, and this failure created a need for some means of correcting or supplementing the common law. The common law had become bound by its established forms, procedures, and remedies, and in some cases these could produce results that were unjust or that failed to provide an adequate remedy for a wrong.

The rigid requirements of the common law's forms of action could bar a deserving claim on technical grounds, and the remedies available at common law, which centered on the award of money damages, could be inadequate to provide real justice in cases where what was needed was something other than a payment of money. People who couldn't obtain adequate justice from the common law courts began to seek justice elsewhere, appealing to the king for relief in cases where the common law had failed them, and this appeal to the king for justice beyond the common law became the origin of equity.

These appeals for justice came to be handled by the king's Chancellor, and the Chancellor's handling of these appeals led to the development of equity and of the court that administered it, the Court of Chancery. When people appealed to the king for relief in cases where the common law had failed to provide adequate justice, these appeals came to be referred to the Chancellor, a high royal official, who considered them and provided relief where justice required. The Chancellor, in handling these appeals, wasn't bound by the rigid forms and rules of the common law but could consider what fairness and justice required in the particular circumstances of each case, providing relief on the basis of conscience and fairness where the common law fell short. Over time, the Chancellor's handling of these appeals developed into a regular jurisdiction, and the Court of Chancery emerged as a distinct court administering equity, a body of law and remedies developed to provide justice where the common law was inadequate. Equity thus grew up as a distinct body of law, administered by the Court of Chancery under the Chancellor, alongside the common law administered by the common law courts.

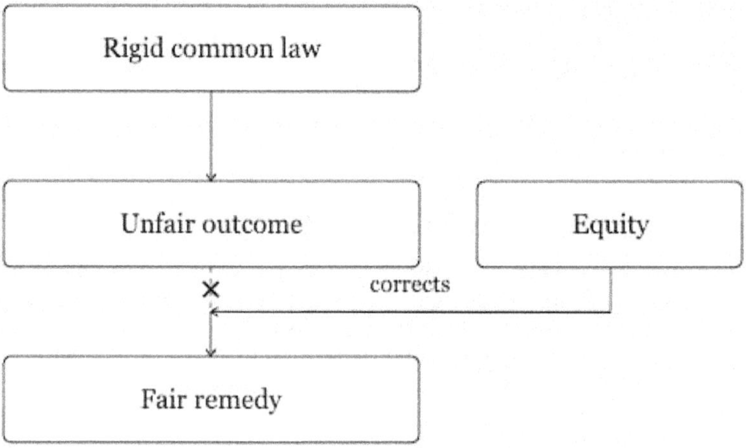

Equity developed its own distinctive principles and remedies, and these were shaped by its origin and purpose as a means of providing justice where the common law fell short. Because equity was concerned with fairness and justice in the particular case, it developed principles oriented toward achieving fair results and toward correcting the inadequacies and unfairnesses that could result from the rigid application of the common law. Equity also developed remedies different from and additional to those available at common law, remedies that could provide justice in cases where the common law's remedy of money damages was inadequate.

Among the most important of these equitable remedies was the injunction, an order of the court requiring a person to do or to refrain from doing something, which could provide justice in situations where preventing or requiring particular conduct was what was needed, rather than merely awarding money. Equity developed other remedies as well, and these equitable remedies expanded the range of relief that the legal system could provide, allowing for justice in cases where the common law's remedies were insufficient. The distinctive principles and remedies of equity made it an important complement to the common law, filling gaps and correcting inadequacies in the ordinary law.

One of equity's most important contributions was the development of the trust, an arrangement that became a significant and distinctive feature of the legal systems descended from English law. The trust is an arrangement in which property is held by one person for the benefit of another, with the person holding the property being bound to use it for the benefit of the person for whom it's held, and equity developed and enforced this arrangement, recognizing and protecting the interests involved. The trust proved to be a valuable and flexible arrangement, useful for a wide range of purposes, and it became an important institution in the law of England and of the nations that inherited the English legal tradition. The development of the trust was one of the significant achievements of equity, and the trust remains an important legal institution in common law systems today, a lasting legacy of the development of equity in English law.

The relationship between equity and the common law was complex, and the two bodies of law existed side by side, administered by different courts, for a long period in the history of English law. For centuries, the common law and equity were administered separately, by the common law courts and the Court of Chancery respectively, each with its own body of law, its own principles, and its own remedies. This separate administration of law and equity was a distinctive feature of the English legal system, and it meant that the legal system comprised two bodies of law working alongside each other, with equity supplementing and correcting the common law. In later times, reforms brought about a merging of the administration of law and equity, so that the same courts came to administer both, but the distinction between legal and equitable principles and remedies remained significant, and the body of equity developed through the Court of Chancery remained an important part of the law. The development of equity alongside the common law gave the English legal tradition a distinctive dual character, with equity providing a means of achieving justice and fairness where the common law alone was inadequate, and the legacy of equity remains an important part of the legal systems descended from English law.

Contrasting the common law and equity, the two bodies of law that together formed the English legal tradition.

Feature	Common Law	Equity
Origin	Royal courts and their decisions	Appeals to the king, handled by the Chancellor
Administered by	The common law courts	The Court of Chancery
Guiding concern	Established rules, forms, and precedent	Fairness and justice in the particular case
Typical remedy	Money damages	Injunctions, specific performance, the trust

Character	More fixed and rule-bound	More flexible, focused on conscience

The Statute of Westminster and early parliamentary legislation

Alongside the judge-made common law and the equity administered by the Court of Chancery, another source of law grew in importance during the medieval and later periods: legislation, the making of law by statute, and particularly the making of law by Parliament. The development of legislation as a source of law was significant, introducing a means of making law that differed from the development of law through judicial decisions, and over time legislation would grow to become the dominant source of law in the modern age.

Understanding the emergence of legislation, including early statutes and the development of Parliament's role in making law, is important for understanding the sources of law in the English legal tradition and the changing balance among them over time.

In the earlier development of the common law, law had developed principally through the decisions of the royal judges, building up the body of the common law case by case. But law could also be made more directly, through the issuing of legislation, statutes that laid down law by deliberate enactment rather than through the gradual accumulation of judicial decisions. Early legislation included statutes enacted by the king, sometimes with the counsel and consent of the great men of the realm, addressing various matters and laying down rules of law. Among the significant early statutes were the Statutes of Westminster, important pieces of medieval English legislation that addressed various matters of law and made significant provisions affecting the law of the kingdom. These early statutes represented the making of law by deliberate enactment, a source of law alongside the judge-made common law, and they contributed to the development of the law of England.

Over time, the making of legislation came to be associated increasingly with Parliament, and the development of Parliament's role in making law was a development of great importance for the English legal and constitutional tradition. Parliament developed over the medieval period as an institution representing, in some measure, the community of the realm, and it came to play an increasingly important role in the making of law, so that legislation came to be enacted by Parliament, in a process involving the different elements of Parliament along with the crown. The development of Parliament's role in making law meant that legislation, the deliberate enactment of law by statute, came to be the function of Parliament, and the growth of Parliament's legislative role was a significant development in the English legal and constitutional system. Over the long course of English constitutional history, Parliament's role in making law would grow in importance, and Parliament would come to be recognized as the supreme law-making authority, whose legislation was the highest form of law.

The emergence of legislation as a source of law, and the development of Parliament's role in making it, introduced an important element into the English legal system and affected the balance among the sources of law. With legislation as a source of law, alongside the judge-made common law and the equity of the Court of Chancery, the English legal system comprised multiple sources of law, and the relationship among these sources became an important feature of the legal system. Legislation could change the law, laying down new rules by deliberate enactment and altering or overriding the rules established by the common law, and this gave legislation a distinctive power to change and shape the law directly. As legislation grew in importance over time, and as Parliament's legislative role and authority developed, legislation came to be an increasingly significant source of law, and in the modern age legislation would become the dominant source of law, with the judge-made common law operating alongside and beneath the framework established by legislation.

The development of legislation and of Parliament's law-making role points toward the modern relationship among the sources of law, in which legislation enacted by the legislature is the primary source of law, while the judge-made common law continues to operate in the areas not governed by legislation and in the interpretation and application of the law.

In the modern common law systems descended from the English legal tradition, legislation and the common law work together, with legislation as the supreme source of law, capable of changing the law by enactment, and the common law continuing to develop through judicial decisions in the areas not covered by legislation and in the interpretation of statutes and the application of the law to cases. This relationship between legislation and the common law, in which both are sources of law with legislation supreme, is a characteristic feature of the modern common law systems, and it developed over the long history of English law through the emergence and growth of legislation alongside the judge-made common law. The rise of legislation, beginning with early statutes and developing through the growth of Parliament's law-making role, was thus a development of lasting importance, shaping the sources of law in the common law tradition and establishing the framework within which law is made and developed in the common law systems of the modern world.

Discussion question: The English legal tradition ended up with two bodies of law, the rigid common law and the more flexible equity, precisely because a single system built on fixed rules kept producing unfair results in particular cases. This suggests a permanent tension in law between consistency, which requires firm rules applied the same way every time, and fairness, which sometimes requires bending or setting aside the rules to fit the circumstances. Can any legal system fully resolve this tension, or is the need for something like equity, some escape valve from the rigidity of rules, a permanent feature of any system that takes both consistency and fairness seriously?

Chapter 9: Legal Revolutions of the 17th and 18th Centuries

The seventeenth and eighteenth centuries changed the world's understanding of law and government more profoundly than any period since ancient Greece. In these two centuries, thinkers and revolutionaries put forward new ideas about the source of governmental authority, the rights of individuals, and the proper structure of government, and they translated these ideas into revolutions, constitutions, and legal reforms that reshaped the political and legal landscape.

The old assumption that kings ruled by divine right and that subjects owed them obedience gave way to new ideas: that government derives its authority from the consent of the governed, that individuals possess rights that governments must respect, and that governmental power must be structured and limited to protect liberty. These ideas, worked out by philosophers and put into practice by revolutionaries, became the foundation of modern constitutional government and modern ideas about law and rights.

This was an age of revolution in both thought and action. On the level of thought, philosophers developed powerful new theories about the nature and origin of government, the rights of individuals, and the foundations of political authority, theories that challenged the old order and provided the intellectual foundation for a new understanding of law and government.

On the level of action, revolutions and reforms transformed the actual institutions of government and law, establishing new systems based on the new ideas and sweeping away or transforming the old order. The combination of revolutionary thought and revolutionary action makes this one of the most consequential periods in the history of law, a period that produced many of the fundamental ideas and institutions of modern constitutional government and modern legal systems.

The developments of these centuries have shaped the law and government of much of the world down to the present day. The ideas about consent, rights, and limited government that emerged in this period became the foundation of modern constitutional democracy, and the specific institutions and documents produced by the revolutions and reforms of the age, the constitutions, the declarations of rights, the legal codes, became models that influenced the development of law and government around the world. To understand modern constitutional government, modern ideas about rights, and modern legal systems, we must understand the revolutions in thought and action of the seventeenth and eighteenth centuries, which laid the foundations of the modern legal and political order.

Hobbes, Locke, and Rousseau on law and the social contract

The intellectual foundation of the legal and political revolutions of the seventeenth and eighteenth centuries was laid by a group of philosophers who developed new theories about the origin and nature of government, and among the most important of these were the theories built around the idea of the social contract. The social contract theorists sought to explain the origin and basis of government and political authority by imagining how government might have arisen from an original condition in which there was no government, and by conceiving of government as based on a kind of agreement or contract. Three thinkers in particular, Thomas Hobbes, John Locke, and Jean-Jacques Rousseau, developed influential versions of social contract theory, and their ideas profoundly shaped modern thinking about law, government, and political authority, though they reached notably different conclusions.

The social contract theorists typically began by imagining a condition in which there was no government, often called the state of nature, and by asking what such a condition would be like and why people would establish a government to escape it. By conceiving of an original condition without government and asking how and why government would arise from it, the social contract theorists sought to explain the basis and purpose of government and to establish principles about what government should be and what its limits should be. The idea was that government arose, or could be understood as arising, from an agreement among people to establish a government for their common benefit, and that this agreement, the social contract, was the basis of governmental authority and defined the purposes and limits of government. Different theorists imagined the state of nature differently and drew different conclusions about the resulting government, but the common framework of the state of nature and the social contract provided a powerful way of thinking about the basis and purpose of government.

Thomas Hobbes, writing in the seventeenth century against the background of the upheavals and civil conflict of his time in England, developed a version of social contract theory that emphasized the need for strong government to secure peace and order. Hobbes imagined the state of nature, the condition without government, as a condition of insecurity, conflict, and danger, in which the absence of a common authority to keep order would lead to a war of all against all, making life insecure and miserable.

In Hobbes's famous description, life in such a condition would be poor, unpleasant, and short, lacking the security and benefits that only an ordered society under government could provide. From this grim picture of the state of nature, Hobbes argued that people would agree to establish a government, submitting to a strong sovereign authority in order to escape the insecurity and conflict of the state of nature and to secure peace and order. Hobbes's theory thus provided a justification for strong government, emphasizing the need for a powerful sovereign authority to maintain order and security and to save people from the dangers of a condition without government.

John Locke, writing later in the seventeenth century, developed a version of social contract theory that proved enormously influential for the development of liberal and constitutional ideas about government, and Locke's ideas deserve particular attention for their profound influence on modern constitutional and liberal thought. Locke imagined the state of nature differently from Hobbes, conceiving of it not as a condition of sheer war and chaos but as a condition in which people possessed certain natural rights, including rights to life, liberty, and property, though lacking the security and impartial enforcement that government could provide. For Locke, people possessed these natural rights by nature, prior to and independent of government, and the purpose of government was to protect these rights, to provide the security and impartial enforcement of rights that the state of nature lacked. People established government, in Locke's theory, in order to better protect their natural rights, and government therefore existed for the purpose of protecting the rights of the people and derived its authority from the consent of the governed.

Locke's theory had profound implications for ideas about the limits of government and the rights of the people, implications that made it a foundation of liberal and constitutional thought. Because government existed to protect the rights of the people and derived its authority from their consent, government was limited by its purpose and by the consent on which it rested, and a government that failed to protect the people's rights, or that violated them, betrayed the very purpose for which it was established. Locke argued that the people had the right to alter or replace a government that violated their rights and betrayed its trust, a principle that provided a justification for resistance to tyrannical government and for the alteration or replacement of governments that failed in their purpose. Locke's ideas, emphasizing natural rights, government by consent, the limitation of government by its purpose of protecting rights, and the right of the people to resist or replace a government that violated its trust, became a foundation of liberal and constitutional thought, and they profoundly influenced the political and legal revolutions of the age, including the American Revolution and the ideas embodied in the founding documents of the United States.

Jean-Jacques Rousseau, writing in the eighteenth century, developed a version of social contract theory that emphasized ideas about popular sovereignty and the general will, and his ideas had a significant influence on political thought, including on the ideas associated with the French Revolution. Rousseau's theory conceived of the social contract as the basis of a political community in which the people were sovereign, and he developed the idea of the general will, the collective will of the people directed toward the common good, as the basis of legitimate law and government. For Rousseau, legitimate government and law were based on the general will of the people, and the people, as sovereign, were the ultimate source of legitimate political authority. Rousseau's emphasis on popular sovereignty, on the people as the source of legitimate authority, and on the general will as the basis of legitimate law, influenced the development of democratic and republican ideas, and his thought was associated with the more radical and democratic currents of the political thought of the age, including ideas that found expression in the French Revolution.

Comparing the three great social contract theorists and the different conclusions they drew from a common framework.

Thinker	View of the State of Nature	Purpose of Government	Key Idea
Hobbes	Insecure, a war of all against all	To secure peace and order	A strong sovereign is needed to escape chaos
Locke	People hold natural rights but lack protection	To protect life, liberty, and property	Government rests on consent and may be replaced if it fails
Rousseau	A starting point for a sovereign community	To express the general will of the people	The people are sovereign; law rests on the general will

The social contract theorists, despite their differences, together transformed thinking about the basis and purpose of government, and their collective influence on the development of modern legal and political thought was profound. By conceiving of government as based on agreement and consent rather than on divine right or mere force, and by developing ideas about the natural rights of individuals, the purposes and limits of government, and the sovereignty of the people, the social contract theorists provided a new intellectual foundation for thinking about law and government.

Their ideas challenged the old order, in which kings ruled by divine right and subjects owed obedience, and provided the intellectual basis for a new understanding in which government derived its authority from the people, existed to serve their interests and protect their rights, and was limited and accountable. These ideas became the foundation of modern constitutional and democratic thought, and they profoundly shaped the legal and political revolutions of the seventeenth and eighteenth centuries and the modern legal and political order that emerged from them.

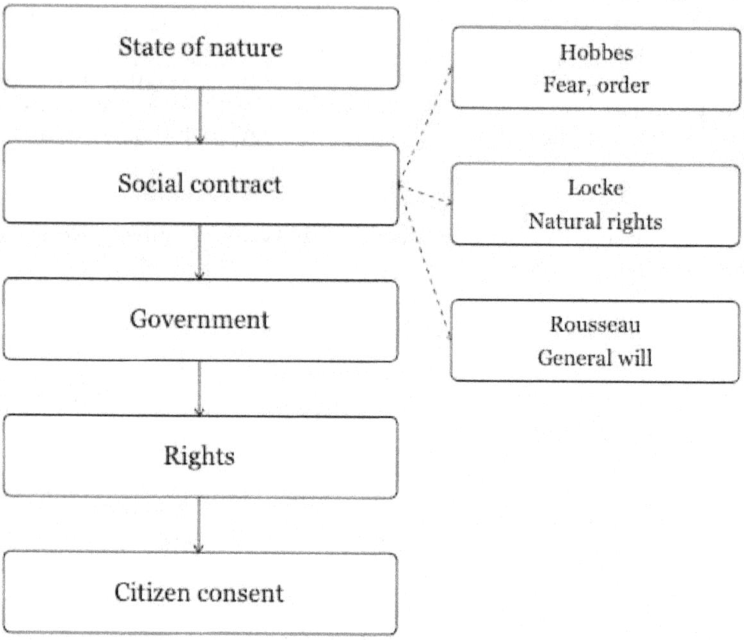

The English Bill of Rights (1689)

England in the seventeenth century was the scene of great constitutional struggles between the crown and Parliament, struggles over the extent of royal power and the rights of Parliament and the people, and these struggles produced important developments in the constitutional and legal order, including the English Bill of Rights of 1689. The Bill of Rights was a significant constitutional document that emerged from these struggles, establishing important principles about the limits of royal power and the rights of Parliament and the people, and it marked an important stage in the development of constitutional government in England. Understanding the Bill of Rights and the struggles from which it emerged is important for understanding the development of constitutional limits on governmental power.

The seventeenth century in England saw prolonged conflict between the crown and Parliament, as kings asserted extensive royal power and Parliament resisted, insisting on its own rights and on limits to royal power. These conflicts included struggles over taxation, over the king's power to govern without Parliament, over religion, and over various assertions of royal authority that Parliament and others resisted as encroachments on their rights and liberties.

The conflicts were severe, including a civil war in the middle of the century and continuing tensions thereafter, and they centered on the fundamental question of the extent of royal power and the rights of Parliament and the people against the crown. These struggles were part of the long development of the English constitution and of the relationship between the crown and Parliament, and they produced important assertions of the rights of Parliament and the people and of limits on royal power.

The English Bill of Rights of 1689 emerged from these struggles as an important settlement establishing constitutional principles, and it came about following the events of the Glorious Revolution, in which a change of monarchs was accompanied by the establishment of constitutional principles limiting royal power.

The Bill of Rights was enacted in the context of this change of monarchs, and it set out important principles about the limits of royal power and the rights of Parliament and the people, principles that the new monarchs accepted and that became part of the constitutional settlement. The Bill of Rights thus represented a significant constitutional settlement, establishing principles that limited the power of the crown and secured the rights of Parliament and the people, and it marked an important development in the movement toward constitutional and limited government in England.

The Bill of Rights established a number of important principles concerning the limits of royal power and the rights of Parliament and the people, and these principles were significant for the development of constitutional government. Among its provisions were principles limiting the power of the crown in various respects, establishing that the crown couldn't exercise certain powers or act in certain ways without the consent of Parliament, and thereby subjecting the exercise of royal power to constitutional limits and to the role of Parliament. The Bill of Rights included provisions concerning the crown's power in relation to law and to taxation, establishing limits on the crown's ability to act in these areas without Parliament, and it thereby secured important aspects of Parliament's role and authority against the assertion of royal power. Through provisions of this kind, the Bill of Rights established constitutional limits on royal power and secured the constitutional role and authority of Parliament, contributing to the development of constitutional and limited government.

The Bill of Rights also included provisions concerning various rights and liberties, contributing to the protection of rights within the constitutional order. It addressed a number of matters concerning the rights and liberties of subjects and the proper conduct of government, establishing principles concerning these matters that formed part of the constitutional settlement. Provisions of the Bill of Rights concerning rights and liberties contributed to the tradition of protecting rights within the English constitutional order, and some of the principles it established had lasting influence, including influence on the development of ideas about rights in other countries. The Bill of Rights thus contributed both to establishing constitutional limits on governmental power and to the protection of rights and liberties within the constitutional order, marking an important development in these respects.

The significance of the English Bill of Rights lies in its contribution to the development of constitutional government and the limitation of governmental power, and it stands as an important document in the history of constitutional government. From establishing constitutional limits on royal power, securing the role and authority of Parliament, and addressing rights and liberties, the Bill of Rights contributed to the development of a constitutional order in which governmental power was limited and subject to constitutional principles and in which the representative institution of Parliament had a secured constitutional role.

This contribution to constitutional and limited government was significant for the development of the English constitution, and it had influence beyond England as well, contributing to the broader development of constitutional government and to ideas about the limitation of governmental power and the protection of rights. The English Bill of Rights, emerging from the constitutional struggles of seventeenth-century England, thus stands as an important document in the development of constitutional government, one that influenced the development of constitutional ideas and documents in other countries, including in America.

The U.S. Constitution and the separation of powers

The founding of the United States produced one of the most influential constitutional documents in the history of the world, the Constitution of the United States, and the constitutional system it established, incorporating ideas about limited government, the separation of powers, and the protection of rights, became a model that profoundly influenced the development of constitutional government around the world. The U.S. Constitution embodied and put into practice many of the ideas about government developed in the preceding period, including ideas about government by consent, limited government, the separation of powers, and the protection of rights, and it created a constitutional system that has endured and that has served as a model for constitutional government elsewhere. Understanding the U.S. Constitution and the principles it embodied is important for understanding the development of modern constitutional government.

The United States Constitution was created following the American Revolution, in which the American colonies had declared and won their independence, and it established the framework of government for the new nation. The Constitution reflected the ideas and experience of the Americans who created it, including the ideas about government developed by the social contract theorists and other thinkers, the experience of the colonists with British rule and their grievances against it, and their own political experience and thought. The Constitution embodied principles about the proper structure and limits of government designed to establish an effective government while guarding against the concentration and abuse of power, reflecting a concern with creating a government that could govern effectively while being limited and preventing tyranny. The Constitution thus represented a deliberate effort to design a system of government based on principles about the proper structure and limits of governmental power.

A central principle embodied in the U.S. Constitution was the separation of powers, the division of governmental power among distinct branches of government, and this principle was fundamental to the constitutional design and to its purpose of preventing the concentration and abuse of power.

Under the principle of the separation of powers, the Constitution divided governmental power among three branches: the legislative branch, which makes the laws; the executive branch, which carries out and enforces the laws; and the judicial branch, which interprets and applies the laws in deciding cases. By dividing governmental power among these three separate branches, each with its own distinct function and its own sphere of authority, the Constitution sought to prevent the concentration of governmental power in any single set of hands, on the reasoning that dividing power among separate branches would guard against the abuse of power and protect liberty. The separation of powers was thus a central feature of the constitutional design, embodying the concern with preventing the concentration and abuse of governmental power.

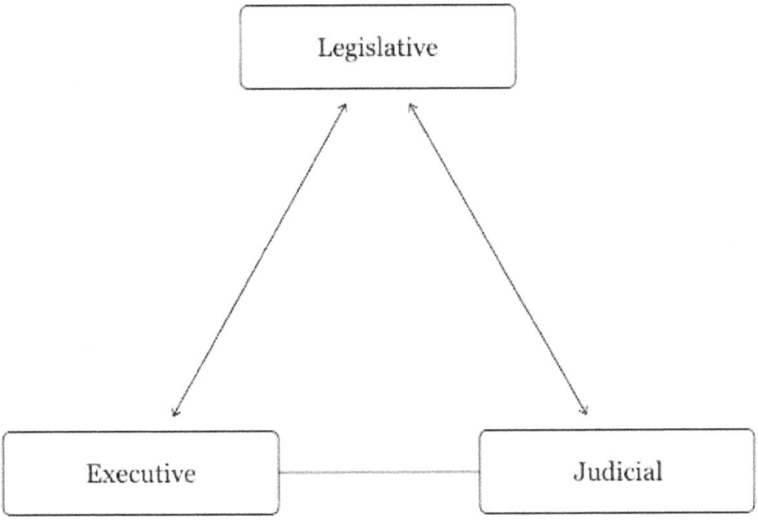

Closely connected with the separation of powers was the system of checks and balances, by which the branches of government were given means of checking one another, and this system reinforced the separation of powers and its purpose of preventing the abuse of power. Under the system of checks and balances, each branch of government was given certain powers to check the others, so that the branches could limit and restrain one another and no branch could dominate or abuse its power without check from the others. This system of mutual checks among the branches was designed to reinforce the separation of powers and to further guard against the concentration and abuse of power, creating a system in which the branches of government would check and balance one another and in which the ambition of each branch would serve to restrain the others. The combination of the separation of powers and the system of checks and balances was central to the constitutional design and to its purpose of establishing a government that was effective yet limited and protected against the abuse of power.

The U.S. Constitution also established a system of federalism, dividing power between the national government and the states, and this division of power was another feature of the constitutional design that contributed to the limitation and distribution of governmental power. Under the federal system established by the Constitution, governmental power was divided between the national or federal government, which had authority over certain matters, and the state governments, which retained authority over other matters, creating a system in which power was distributed between the national and state levels of government. This division of power between the national government and the states was another means of distributing and limiting governmental power, contributing to the overall constitutional design of a government in which power was divided and limited rather than concentrated. Federalism thus added another dimension to the distribution and limitation of governmental power under the Constitution, dividing power not only among the branches of the national government but also between the national government and the states.

An important addition to the U.S. Constitution was the Bill of Rights, the first amendments to the Constitution, which set out protections for various individual rights and liberties, and this addition was significant for the protection of rights within the constitutional system. The Bill of Rights added to the Constitution a set of protections for individual rights and liberties, specifying various rights that were protected against governmental infringement and thereby securing these rights within the constitutional order. The rights protected by the Bill of Rights included various individual freedoms and protections, and by placing these protections in the Constitution, the Bill of Rights secured them as constitutional guarantees, protected against governmental violation and enforceable within the constitutional system. The addition of the Bill of Rights was significant for making the protection of individual rights an explicit part of the constitutional system, and the rights it protected became an important part of the constitutional order, securing individual liberties against governmental infringement.

The table below summarizes the main structural principles of the U.S. Constitution and the purpose each served.

Principle	What It Does	Purpose
Separation of powers	Divides power among legislative, executive, judicial branches	Prevents concentration of power
Checks and balances	Gives each branch means to restrain the others	Guards against abuse of power
Federalism	Divides power between national and state governments	Distributes and limits power
Bill of Rights	Protects specified individual rights and liberties	Secures liberty against government

The U.S. Constitution and the constitutional system it established had enormous influence, both in the United States and around the world, and it stands as one of the most influential constitutional documents in history. Within the United States, the Constitution established a framework of government that has endured and that has provided the basis for the government of the nation over a long history, adapting and developing over time while maintaining its fundamental structure and principles.

Beyond the United States, the Constitution and the principles it embodied, including limited government, the separation of powers, checks and balances, federalism, and the protection of rights, became a model that influenced the development of constitutional government in many other countries, contributing to the spread of constitutional and limited government around the world. The U.S. Constitution thus stands as a landmark in the history of constitutional government, both establishing an enduring system of government in the United States and serving as an influential model for constitutional government elsewhere, embodying and putting into practice many of the ideas about limited and constitutional government that emerged from the revolutions in thought and action of the seventeenth and eighteenth centuries.

The French Revolution and the Napoleonic Code

The French Revolution, which began in 1789, was one of the most momentous events in the history of Europe and the world, and it had a profound impact on law and government, both in France and beyond. The Revolution swept away much of the old order in France and sought to establish a new order based on new principles, including principles about the rights of individuals, the sovereignty of the people, and the reform of law and government, and it produced important developments in law, including a famous declaration of rights and, later, the Napoleonic Code, one of the most influential legal codes in history. Understanding the French Revolution and its impact on law, including the Napoleonic Code, is important for understanding the development of modern law, particularly in the civil law tradition.

The French Revolution arose from deep discontent with the old order in France, an order marked by absolute monarchy, social inequality and privilege, and various grievances that had built up among the population. The Revolution swept away much of this old order, abolishing many of its institutions and features, including feudal privileges and the absolute power of the monarchy, and it sought to establish a new order based on new principles.

Among the ideas that animated the Revolution were principles about the rights of individuals, the equality of citizens, the sovereignty of the people, and the reform of the institutions of government and law, ideas that reflected the influence of the political thought of the preceding period, including the ideas of the social contract theorists and other thinkers of the Enlightenment. The Revolution thus represented a profound break with the old order and an effort to establish a new order based on new principles about government, law, and the rights of individuals.

One of the important early products of the French Revolution was the Declaration of the Rights of Man and of the Citizen, a document that set out fundamental principles about the rights of individuals, and this declaration was significant for the assertion of individual rights and for its influence on the development of ideas about rights. The Declaration of the Rights of Man and of the Citizen, adopted in the early period of the Revolution, proclaimed various fundamental rights of individuals and principles about government and law, asserting principles about the natural rights of individuals, the equality of citizens, and the proper basis and purpose of government and law. The Declaration reflected the influence of natural rights theory and the political thought of the Enlightenment, and it asserted principles about the rights of individuals and the proper basis of government that were significant both for the Revolution and for the broader development of ideas about rights. The

Declaration became an influential statement of principles about individual rights, and it had a lasting influence on the development of ideas about human rights, standing as an important document in the history of the assertion and protection of individual rights.

The most influential legal product to emerge from the period of the French Revolution and its aftermath was the Napoleonic Code, a comprehensive codification of French civil law enacted under Napoleon, and this code became one of the most influential legal codes in history, profoundly shaping the development of law in the civil law tradition. The Napoleonic Code was a systematic and comprehensive codification of the civil law, the law governing such matters as persons, property, contracts, and other matters of private law, organizing this law into a clear, systematic, and comprehensive code. The Code reflected principles associated with the Revolution and its aftermath, including principles about the equality of citizens before the law and the establishment of a uniform law applying throughout the nation, replacing the varied and complex legal arrangements of the old order with a single, systematic, and uniform code. The Napoleonic Code was a landmark in the development of law, providing a model of comprehensive legal codification and embodying principles about law that were significant for the development of modern legal systems.

The influence of the Napoleonic Code was enormous, extending far beyond France and profoundly shaping the development of law in the civil law tradition around the world, and this influence makes the Code one of the most important developments in the history of law. The Napoleonic Code became a model for legal codification, and its systematic and comprehensive codification of the civil law influenced the development of legal codes in many other countries, spreading the model of comprehensive codification and the principles embodied in the Code. Through the influence of the Napoleonic Code, and through the spread of French law and legal ideas, the Code shaped the development of the civil law systems of many nations, contributing to the development of the civil law tradition as it exists in much of the world today. The Napoleonic Code thus stands as a landmark in the history of law, a highly influential model of legal codification that profoundly shaped the development of the civil law tradition, and its influence continues to be felt in the legal systems of many nations that were influenced by it. In this way, the French Revolution, through the Napoleonic Code and the Declaration of the Rights of Man, had a profound and lasting impact on the development of modern law, both in the assertion of individual rights and in the codification of law in the civil law tradition.

Natural rights theory and its effect on legal reform

Running through the legal and political revolutions of the seventeenth and eighteenth centuries was a powerful idea that gave much of the period its distinctive character and that had a profound effect on legal reform: the theory of natural rights. Natural rights theory held that individuals possess certain rights by nature, rights that belong to them as human beings prior to and independent of government, and that these natural rights ought to be respected and protected by government and law. This idea, which built on the older tradition of natural law that we've traced from the ancient world, became a driving force behind the assertion of individual rights and the reform of law and government in this period, and it had a lasting effect on the development of modern law and modern ideas about rights.

Natural rights theory developed from the older tradition of natural law, the idea of a higher law grounded in nature or reason, but it gave this tradition a new emphasis on the rights of individuals. Where the older natural law tradition had emphasized a higher law or standard of justice above human law, natural rights theory emphasized the rights that individuals possess by nature, conceiving of individuals as bearers of natural rights that belong to them as human beings and that government and law ought to respect and protect.

This emphasis on the natural rights of individuals was developed by thinkers of the period, notably including John Locke, whose theory conceived of individuals as possessing natural rights to life, liberty, and property prior to and independent of government, and whose ideas about natural rights profoundly influenced the political and legal thought of the age. The development of natural rights theory, with its emphasis on the rights that individuals possess by nature, gave the natural law tradition a new focus on individual rights that was significant for the developments of the period.

Natural rights theory had a powerful effect on the assertion of rights and the reform of law and government, providing a foundation for claims about the rights of individuals and for the reform of law and government to respect and protect these rights. The idea that individuals possess natural rights that government and law ought to respect and protect provided a basis for asserting rights against government and for demanding that government and law be reformed to respect and protect these rights, and it thereby became a driving force behind the assertion of rights and the reform of law and government in this period. Natural rights theory provided the intellectual foundation for the assertions of rights in the great documents of the period, including the assertion of rights in the founding documents of the United States and in the French Declaration of the Rights of Man and of the Citizen, both of which reflected the influence of natural rights theory and its emphasis on the rights that individuals possess by nature. Through its influence on these documents and on the broader political and legal thought and action of the period, natural rights theory had a profound effect on the assertion of rights and the reform of law and government.

The effect of natural rights theory on legal reform was significant and far-reaching, contributing to reforms in law and government designed to respect and protect the rights of individuals. The idea that individuals possess natural rights that ought to be respected and protected provided a basis and a motivation for reforming law and government to better respect and protect these rights, and it contributed to various reforms in this period and beyond. Reforms influenced by natural rights theory included the establishment of protections for individual rights in constitutions and declarations, the reform of laws and legal institutions to respect the rights and equality of individuals, and the movement toward legal systems that recognized and protected the rights of individuals. Natural rights theory thus contributed to a broad movement of legal reform aimed at establishing law and government that respected and protected the natural rights of individuals, and this movement had a lasting effect on the development of modern legal systems and their protection of individual rights.

The legacy of natural rights theory has been enduring, and its influence continues to be felt in modern law and modern ideas about rights, particularly in the development of the concept of human rights. The idea that individuals possess rights by virtue of their humanity, which natural rights theory developed and asserted, became a foundation for the modern concept of human rights, the idea that all human beings possess certain fundamental rights simply by virtue of being human, rights that ought to be respected and protected everywhere. The natural rights theory of the seventeenth and eighteenth centuries thus contributed to the development of the modern concept of human rights, and its emphasis on the rights that individuals possess by nature has had a lasting influence on modern law and modern ideas about rights.

In this way, natural rights theory, which drew on the ancient tradition of natural law and gave it a new emphasis on individual rights, had a profound and lasting effect not only on the legal reforms of its own period but on the development of modern law and modern ideas about human rights, standing as one of the most influential ideas in the history of law and of the assertion and protection of individual rights.

Discussion question: The revolutions of this era grounded government in the consent of the governed and in natural rights that belong to all people, yet the same societies that proclaimed these universal principles often denied rights to large portions of their own populations, holding people in slavery and excluding many from the political community even as they declared all people to possess natural rights. Was this contradiction a betrayal that exposed the principles as hollow, or did the very act of proclaiming universal rights plant a standard that could later be used to challenge and overturn the exclusions, and what does this tell us about the relationship between the ideals a legal system proclaims and the injustices it tolerates in practice?

Chapter 10: Modern Legal Systems and International Law

We've traveled a long way, from disputes settled around a fire in prehistoric times to codes carved in stone, from the courts of Athens and Rome to the legal systems of medieval Europe and the Islamic world, and through the revolutions in thought and law that gave birth to modern constitutional government.

Now we arrive at the present, at the legal systems that govern our world today and at the new forms of law that have arisen to meet the challenges of a connected and rapidly changing global society. This final chapter surveys the modern legal landscape, examining the great legal traditions that govern the nations of the world, the development of law among nations, the rise of human rights and international justice, and the new challenges that confront law in an age of technology and global interconnection.

The modern world inherited the great legal traditions we've traced through this book, and these traditions continue to shape the law of the nations of the world today. The two great families of legal systems that emerged from the history we've followed, the civil law tradition descended from Roman law and the common law tradition originating in England, govern the law of most of the world's nations, and understanding these traditions and their differences is essential to understanding the legal systems of the modern world.

But the modern age has also seen the development of new forms of law that go beyond the law of individual nations, including the development of international law governing relations among nations, the rise of human rights law asserting the rights of all human beings, and the establishment of international justice for the gravest crimes. And the modern world confronts new challenges that test the capacity of law to keep pace with a changing world, including challenges arising from new technologies and from the increasing interconnection of a globalized world.

This chapter brings our history up to the present and looks toward the future, examining both the enduring legal traditions that govern the modern world and the new developments and challenges that are shaping the law of our time. In doing so, it completes our survey of the evolution of legal systems, from the earliest origins of law to the complex legal order of the contemporary world, and it points toward the questions and challenges that will shape the continuing development of law in the years to come. The story of law doesn't end here, for law continues to develop and change as it always has, but this chapter brings us to the present moment in that long and continuing story.

Civil law versus common law systems today

The nations of the world today are governed by legal systems that belong, for the most part, to one of two great legal traditions, the civil law tradition and the common law tradition, and these two traditions, whose origins we've traced through this book, are the dominant legal families of the modern world. Understanding the distinction between the civil law and common law traditions, and the characteristics of each, is essential to understanding the legal systems of the modern world, because the legal system of most nations reflects one or the other of these traditions, and the differences between them shape the character of law and legal practice in different parts of the world. While there are other legal traditions in the world as well, including systems based on religious law and various other traditions, the civil law and common law traditions are the two most widespread and influential, governing the law of a large majority of the world's nations.

The civil law tradition, which we've traced from its origins in Roman law through its preservation in Justinian's compilation and its development in continental Europe, is the more widespread of the two traditions, governing the law of much of the world. The civil law tradition is characterized above all by its reliance on comprehensive legal codes, systematic and comprehensive statements of the law enacted as legislation, which serve as the primary source of law.

In civil law systems, the law is found principally in these comprehensive codes, which aim to set out the law systematically and comprehensively, and the role of the judge is understood principally as applying and interpreting the code to decide cases, rather than as making law through decisions. The civil law tradition, with its reliance on comprehensive codes and its systematic approach to law, descended from Roman law and was shaped by the revival of Roman legal study in medieval Europe and by developments such as the Napoleonic Code, and it spread to much of the world, governing the law of continental Europe, Latin America, and many other regions.

The common law tradition, which we've traced from its origins in medieval England, is the other great legal tradition of the modern world, and it differs from the civil law tradition in important respects that reflect its distinctive origins and character. **The common law tradition is characterized by its reliance on judicial decisions and precedent as a primary source of law**, with the law developing through the decisions of judges in cases and with past decisions serving as precedents that guide the decision of future cases under the principle of stare decisis. In common law systems, the role of the judge is understood as including a role in developing and shaping the law through decisions, and the law is found in significant part in the accumulated decisions of the courts, alongside legislation. The common law tradition, with its reliance on judicial decisions and precedent and its distinctive role for the judge, originated in medieval England and spread to many parts of the world through English influence, governing the law of England and of many nations whose legal systems descend from the English common law.

The differences between the civil law and common law traditions are significant, and they shape the character of law and legal practice in the nations governed by each tradition, though it's important to recognize that the differences shouldn't be overstated and that the two traditions have influenced and converged with each other in various ways. The principal differences concern the primary sources of law, with civil law systems relying principally on comprehensive codes and common law systems relying significantly on judicial decisions and precedent, and the role of the judge, with the civil law judge understood principally as applying and interpreting the code and the common law judge understood as also developing the law through decisions. These differences affect various aspects of law and legal practice, including how the law is found and stated, how legal reasoning proceeds, and how the law develops, giving the legal systems of the two traditions somewhat different characters. At the same time, the two traditions share much in common, both being sophisticated legal systems addressing the same fundamental legal problems, and they have influenced each other and converged in various respects, with civil law systems making use of judicial decisions and common law systems making extensive use of legislation, so that the differences between them, while significant, aren't absolute.

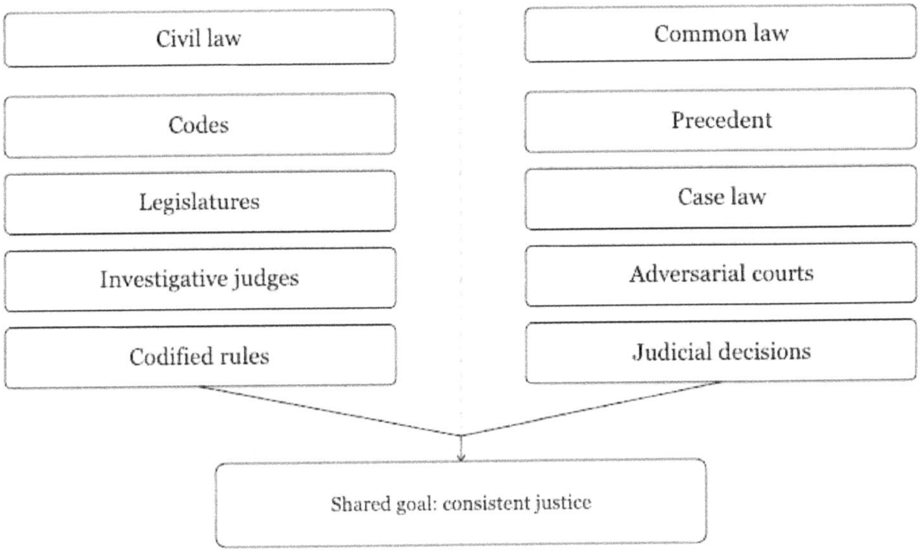

The distribution of the two traditions across the world reflects the historical processes by which they spread, and it has resulted in a world in which most nations are governed by one or the other of the two traditions, with some nations combining elements of both.

The civil law tradition spread from continental Europe to Latin America, to parts of Africa and Asia, and to other regions, largely through the influence of the European nations whose law belonged to the civil law tradition, and it governs the law of a large number of nations. The common law tradition spread from England to many parts of the world that came under English influence, and it governs the law of England and of many other nations with historical connections to England. Some nations combine elements of both traditions, or combine one of these traditions with other legal traditions such as religious law, resulting in mixed legal systems that draw on more than one tradition. The result is a world in which the civil law and common law traditions, whose long histories we've traced, are the dominant legal families, governing the law of most of the world's nations and shaping the character of law and legal practice around the world.

The table below summarizes the main differences between the two great legal traditions that govern most of the modern world.

Feature	Civil Law	Common Law
Primary source of law	Comprehensive codes	Judicial decisions and precedent
Role of the judge	Applies and interprets the code	Develops law through decisions
Historical origin	Roman law, revived and codified	Medieval English royal justice
Role of precedent	Less binding; codes are primary	Central (stare decisis)
Where it predominates	Continental Europe, Latin America, and beyond	England and nations of English legal heritage

The formation of international law from Westphalia to the UN

The legal systems we've discussed so far are the legal systems of individual nations, governing the affairs within each nation, but the modern world also has a body of law that governs the relations among nations, international law, and the development of international law is an important part of the story of law in the modern world. International law is the body of law that governs the relations among nations and other actors in the international community, addressing such matters as the conduct of nations toward one another, the making and effect of treaties and agreements among nations, and various other matters concerning the international community. The development of international law, from its early modern origins to the more developed international legal order of the present, is an important development in the history of law, reflecting the growth of a legal order governing the relations among the nations of the world.

An important development in the history of the modern international order is often associated with the Peace of Westphalia in the seventeenth century, which is frequently taken as a landmark in the development of the modern system of sovereign states, and understanding this development helps in understanding the framework within which international law developed. The Peace of Westphalia, which ended a major European conflict in the seventeenth century, is often regarded as a significant point in the development of the modern system of sovereign states, the system in which the world is organized into sovereign states, each with authority over its own territory and affairs, and in which the international order is understood as an order among these sovereign states. This system of sovereign states became the framework within which the modern international order and international law developed, with international law understood as the law governing the relations among these sovereign states. The association of the Peace of Westphalia with the development of the modern system of sovereign states reflects the importance of this system as the framework of the modern international order, within which international law developed as the law governing relations among sovereign states.

The development of international law involved the growth of a body of law and principles governing the relations among nations, developed over time through various sources and processes, and this development produced an increasingly elaborate body of international law over the modern period. International law developed through various sources, including the practice of nations in their relations with one another, the agreements and treaties made among nations, the writings of scholars of international law, and other sources, and through these sources a body of international law developed governing various aspects of the relations among nations.

Early scholars of international law made important contributions to its development, articulating principles about the law governing the relations among nations and helping to establish international law as a field of law and study. Over time, international law grew into an increasingly elaborate body of law, addressing an expanding range of matters concerning the relations among nations and the conduct of nations in the international community, and it became an established, if distinctive, body of law governing the international order.

A major development in the international legal order in the modern period was the establishment of international organizations, and particularly the establishment of the United Nations following the Second World War, which marked an important development in the international order and in international law. The United Nations was established after the Second World War as an international organization intended to maintain international peace and security and to promote cooperation among nations, and its establishment marked an important development in the international order, creating a major international organization with broad purposes and a significant role in international affairs.

The establishment of the United Nations and of the broader framework of international organizations and institutions in the modern period contributed to the development of a more elaborate international order, with international organizations playing significant roles in international affairs and in the development and application of international law. The United Nations became a central institution in the modern international order, with a significant role in matters of international peace and security and in the promotion of international cooperation, and its establishment was an important development in the modern international legal order.

The character of international law is distinctive, and it differs in important respects from the law within nations, in ways that reflect the nature of the international order as an order among sovereign states. Unlike the law within a nation, which is made and enforced by the government of the nation with authority over those within it, international law governs the relations among sovereign states, and it lacks a single overarching government with authority over the nations to make and enforce law in the way that a national government does within a nation. This gives international law a distinctive character, as a body of law governing the relations among sovereign states in the absence of a single overarching government over them, and it raises distinctive questions about how international law is made, how it's enforced, and how it functions as law. Despite these distinctive features and the questions they raise, international law is an established body of law that governs important aspects of the relations among nations and that plays a significant role in the international order, even as its distinctive character, as law among sovereign states rather than law within a nation under a government, distinguishes it from the law within nations and gives it a particular character and particular challenges.

Human rights law and the Universal Declaration (1948)

One of the most significant developments in the law of the modern world has been the rise of human rights law, the body of law concerned with the rights that belong to all human beings, and the development of human rights law represents an important chapter in the modern history of law and in the long history of ideas about rights that we've traced through this book. Human rights law is concerned with the fundamental rights that are held to belong to all human beings simply by virtue of their humanity, rights that ought to be respected and protected everywhere, and its development in the modern period, particularly following the Second World War, marked an important development in the assertion and protection of these rights at the international level. The rise of human rights law drew on the long tradition of ideas about natural law and natural rights that we've traced, giving these ideas a new form and a new prominence in the modern international order.

The idea of human rights, the idea that all human beings possess certain fundamental rights by virtue of their humanity, has roots in the long tradition of ideas about natural law and natural rights that we've traced through this book, from the ancient idea of a natural law common to all humanity, through the natural rights theory of the seventeenth and eighteenth centuries, to the modern concept of human rights.

The modern concept of human rights builds on this long tradition, taking up the idea that human beings possess fundamental rights by virtue of their humanity and developing it into the modern concept of human rights held to belong to all human beings everywhere. The development of the modern concept of human rights, drawing on this long tradition of ideas about the rights of human beings, gave these ideas a new form and a new prominence, and it became the basis for the development of human rights law in the modern period, asserting and seeking to protect the fundamental rights of all human beings.

A landmark in the development of modern human rights was the adoption of the Universal Declaration of Human Rights in 1948, following the Second World War, and this document was a document of great significance in the history of human rights and in the assertion of the rights of all human beings. The Universal Declaration of Human Rights, adopted by the United Nations in 1948, set out a broad range of fundamental human rights held to belong to all human beings, proclaiming these rights as a common standard for all peoples and nations. The Declaration was adopted in the aftermath of the Second World War, a conflict that had involved terrible atrocities and violations of human rights, and it reflected a determination to assert and protect the fundamental rights of all human beings in response to these violations. The Universal Declaration proclaimed a wide range of human rights, encompassing various civil, political, economic, social, and cultural rights, and it asserted these rights as belonging to all human beings and as a common standard to be respected and protected. The adoption of the Universal Declaration of Human Rights was a landmark in the history of human rights, a significant assertion of the fundamental rights of all human beings at the international level, and it became a foundational document in the modern development of human rights.

The Universal Declaration of Human Rights had great influence, and it became the foundation for the further development of human rights law and for the assertion and protection of human rights in the modern world. Following the adoption of the Universal Declaration, human rights law developed further through various international agreements and instruments that set out human rights in binding legal form, building on the foundation the Declaration provided and developing an increasingly elaborate body of international human rights law. These developments included the adoption of international treaties and agreements on human rights, which set out human rights in the form of binding legal obligations and established various mechanisms concerning the protection of human rights, and the development of various institutions and mechanisms concerned with human rights at the international and regional levels. Through these developments, building on the foundation of the Universal Declaration, an increasingly elaborate body of international human rights law developed, asserting and seeking to protect the fundamental rights of all human beings and establishing human rights as an important part of the modern international legal order.

The development of human rights law represents a significant development in the modern history of law, and it reflects the assertion of the fundamental rights of all human beings as a matter of international concern and law. The rise of human rights law established the idea that the fundamental rights of human beings are a matter of international concern, that these rights ought to be respected and protected everywhere, and that their violation is a matter of concern to the international community, not merely a matter internal to individual nations. This represented a significant development, asserting the fundamental rights of all human beings at the international level and establishing human rights as an important part of the modern international legal order.

At the same time, the protection of human rights in practice faces significant challenges, and the assertion of human rights in law doesn't by itself ensure their protection in practice, so that the gap between the assertion of human rights and their actual protection remains a significant challenge in the modern world. Despite these challenges, the development of human rights law represents a significant development in the modern history of law, establishing the fundamental rights of all human beings as a matter of international law and concern and giving new form and prominence to the long tradition of ideas about the rights of human beings that we've traced through this book.

The International Criminal Court and war crimes prosecution

Among the significant developments in the modern international legal order has been the development of international criminal justice, the prosecution of individuals for the gravest crimes of international concern, and this development, including the establishment of the International Criminal Court, represents an important development in international law and in the effort to hold individuals accountable for the gravest crimes. International criminal justice is concerned with the prosecution and punishment of individuals for certain grave crimes of international concern, such as war crimes, crimes against humanity, and genocide, crimes so grave that they're regarded as matters of concern to the international community as a whole. The development of international criminal justice, including the prosecution of individuals for such crimes and the establishment of institutions for this purpose, represents a significant development in the modern international legal order, extending the reach of law to hold individuals accountable for the gravest crimes.

An important development in the emergence of international criminal justice came in the aftermath of the Second World War, with the prosecution of individuals for grave crimes committed during the war, and these prosecutions were significant precedents for the development of international criminal justice. Following the Second World War, international tribunals were established to prosecute individuals for grave crimes committed during the war, including war crimes, crimes against humanity, and crimes against peace, and these prosecutions held individuals accountable for their roles in the grave crimes of the war. These post-war prosecutions were significant developments, establishing important precedents for the prosecution of individuals for grave crimes of international concern and for the principle that individuals could be held accountable under international law for such crimes. The post-war tribunals and the principles they established were important precedents for the later development of international criminal justice, contributing to the development of the idea that individuals could be held accountable under international law for the gravest crimes and establishing precedents for the prosecution of such crimes.

A major development in the institutionalization of international criminal justice was the establishment of the International Criminal Court, a permanent international court for the prosecution of the gravest crimes of international concern, and its establishment was a significant development in the effort to hold individuals accountable for such crimes. The International Criminal Court was established as a permanent international court with jurisdiction over certain grave crimes of international concern, including war crimes, crimes against humanity, and genocide, providing a permanent institution for the prosecution of individuals for these gravest crimes. The establishment of the International Criminal Court represented a significant development in international criminal justice, creating a permanent international court for the prosecution of the gravest crimes, in contrast to the earlier tribunals that had been established for particular situations. The International Criminal Court became an institution of the modern international legal order concerned with holding individuals accountable for the gravest crimes of international concern, and its establishment was a significant development in the effort to extend the reach of law and accountability to such crimes.

International criminal justice, including the work of the International Criminal Court, faces significant challenges and limitations, and these challenges are an important part of understanding the development and the reality of international criminal justice in the modern world. International criminal justice operates in the distinctive context of the international order, with its system of sovereign states and its lack of a single overarching government, and this context presents significant challenges for international criminal justice, including challenges concerning the jurisdiction and reach of international criminal justice, the cooperation of states, the enforcement of the decisions of international criminal courts, and the relationship between international criminal justice and the sovereignty of states. These challenges mean that international criminal justice faces significant limitations in practice, and its reach and effectiveness are subject to various constraints arising from the nature of the international order. Despite these challenges and limitations, the development of international criminal justice, including the establishment of the International Criminal Court, represents a significant development in the modern international legal order, extending the principle of accountability under law to individuals for the gravest crimes of international concern and establishing institutions and precedents for holding individuals accountable for such crimes, even as the challenges and limitations it faces remain significant.

Emerging challenges: digital law, AI regulation, and cross-border jurisdiction

The law of the modern world confronts new challenges arising from the rapid changes of the contemporary age, including challenges arising from new technologies and from the increasing interconnection of a globalized world, and these emerging challenges represent the frontier of the continuing development of law in our time. As the world changes, with the development of new technologies and the increasing interconnection of societies and economies across national boundaries, the law faces new challenges and questions that it must address, and the way the law responds to these challenges will shape the continuing development of law in the years to come. These emerging challenges, at the frontier of the law's continuing development, illustrate that the story of law is a continuing one, as law continues to develop and change to meet the challenges of a changing world, just as it has throughout the long history we've traced.

Among the significant emerging challenges for the law are those arising from digital technology and the digital world, which have created new situations and questions that the law must address, and this area of digital law is a rapidly developing area at the frontier of the law's continuing development. The development of digital technology, the internet, and the digital world has created a range of new situations, activities, and questions that the law must address, including questions concerning digital information and data, activity and transactions conducted through digital means, the protection of privacy in the digital age, and many other matters arising from the digital world.

The law has had to develop to address these new situations and questions, and the development of law concerning the digital world is a rapidly developing area, as the law works to address the many new questions and challenges arising from digital technology and the digital world. This area of digital law illustrates the way the law must develop to address the new situations created by technological change, and it's an area of significant and rapid development at the frontier of the law's continuing evolution.

A particularly significant emerging challenge for the law arises from the development of artificial intelligence, which presents new questions and challenges that the law is only beginning to address, and the regulation of artificial intelligence is an area of growing importance at the frontier of the law's development. The development of artificial intelligence, systems capable of performing tasks that would ordinarily require human intelligence, presents a range of new questions and challenges for the law, including questions about how artificial intelligence should be regulated, about responsibility and accountability for the actions and effects of artificial intelligence systems, about the effects of artificial intelligence on various areas of life and law, and about many other matters arising from the development and use of artificial intelligence. These questions are significant and challenging, and the law is only beginning to develop responses to them, as the rapid development of artificial intelligence presents new challenges that the law must work to address. The regulation of artificial intelligence is an area of growing importance and significant challenge, at the frontier of the law's continuing development, and the way the law responds to the challenges presented by artificial intelligence will be an important part of the continuing development of law in the years to come.

Another significant emerging challenge for the law arises from the increasing interconnection of a globalized world and the questions of cross-border jurisdiction and the relations among legal systems that it raises, and these challenges are of growing importance in an interconnected world. The increasing interconnection of societies and economies across national boundaries, with activities, transactions, and relationships increasingly extending across the boundaries of nations and legal systems, raises significant questions about the reach of the law of different nations, about which nation's law applies to activities and matters that cross national boundaries, about the relations and interactions among the legal systems of different nations, and about how legal matters that cross national boundaries should be addressed.

These questions of cross-border jurisdiction and the relations among legal systems are of growing importance in an increasingly interconnected world, as more and more matters extend across national boundaries and raise questions about the reach and application of the law of different nations and about the interactions among different legal systems. The challenges of cross-border jurisdiction and the relations among legal systems in an interconnected world are significant and growing, and addressing them is an important part of the continuing development of law in a globalized world.

Outlining several of the emerging challenges confronting law in the contemporary world and the kinds of questions each raises.

Challenge	Source	Key Questions
Digital law	The internet and digital technology	Data, privacy, digital activity and transactions
AI regulation	Artificial intelligence systems	Regulation, responsibility, accountability, effects
Cross-border jurisdiction	A globalized, interconnected world	Which nation's law applies; how legal systems interact

These emerging challenges illustrate that the development of law is a continuing process, one that continues in our own time as the law works to address the new challenges and questions arising from a changing world, just as it has throughout the long history we've traced through this book. From the earliest origins of law in the disputes of early human societies, through the great codes of the ancient world, the legal traditions of Greece and Rome, the legal systems of medieval Europe and the Islamic world, the revolutions in law and government of the seventeenth and eighteenth centuries, and the modern legal systems and international law of the contemporary world, the story of law has been a story of continuing development, as human societies have developed and adapted law to address the challenges of their circumstances and to pursue justice and order in their affairs.

That story continues in our own time, as the law confronts the new challenges of a changing world, including the challenges arising from new technologies and from the increasing interconnection of a globalized world, and it will continue into the future, as law continues to develop and change to meet the challenges of the times, in the ongoing effort, as old as human society itself, to establish justice, order, and the rule of law in human affairs.

The evolution of legal systems, which we've traced from the ancient codes to the modern world, is a continuing evolution, and the challenges of the present and the future represent the latest chapter in the long and continuing story of the development of law, a story that continues to unfold as human societies continue their ancient effort to govern their affairs through law and to pursue justice under the rule of law.

Discussion question: Throughout this book we've seen law develop slowly, over centuries, as societies gradually worked out how to handle new situations, yet the challenges now arising from technologies like artificial intelligence are developing far faster than law has ever moved, and they cross the national boundaries within which most law is made and enforced. Given that law has always been a relatively slow and largely national response to human problems, is it capable of keeping pace with challenges that are both extremely fast-moving and inherently global, or do these new challenges require us to rethink how law itself is made, and if so, what might a legal system built for a fast-moving and interconnected world need to look like?

Conclusion

We began this book with a black stone pulled from the ground in Iran, carved with the laws of a Babylonian king who lived nearly four thousand years ago. We end it looking at questions about artificial intelligence and law that cross national borders and move faster than any legal system was built to handle. Between those two points lies the whole long story of how human beings learned to govern themselves through law.

What stands out most, looking back over that story, is how the same questions keep returning. What is fair? Who decides? What happens when someone breaks the rules? Should the powerful be bound by the same law as everyone else? People asked these questions around prehistoric fires, in the assemblies of Athens, in the courts of Rome, in medieval villages, and in revolutionary parliaments. They're still being asked today. The answers have changed enormously across the centuries, but the questions have stayed remarkably constant, which tells us something important: law grows out of permanent features of human life, out of our need to live together, resolve our conflicts, and replace violence with order.

We've also seen that law didn't follow a single straight path. The idea that law marches steadily from cruelty toward mercy, or from chaos toward order, doesn't survive contact with the actual history. The oldest written code we have, Ur-Nammu's, relied on payment for injuries, while Hammurabi's later code brought back the eye for an eye. The Hittites softened their laws over time, while the Assyrians kept theirs harsh. Different societies reached different answers, shaped by their own beliefs, circumstances, and values, and the story of law is a story of variety, not a single line of progress.

Certain ideas, once discovered, proved so powerful that they spread and endured. The idea that law should be written and public, so everyone can know it. The idea that the punishment should fit the crime. The idea that even the ruler is bound by law. The idea that people possess rights simply by being human. The idea that agreements should be kept and that the law will enforce them. These ideas emerged at particular moments, in particular places, and then traveled across the centuries, becoming the shared inheritance of much of the world.

The two great legal traditions we followed, the civil law descended from Rome and the common law born in England, now govern most of the world's nations, and alongside them a new body of international law and human rights law has arisen to reach beyond the boundaries of individual nations. Law keeps developing, as it always has.

That's the final lesson of this long history. Law is never finished. It's a living thing, constantly reshaped by human beings trying to build a more just and orderly world. The story that started on that Babylonian stone is still being written, and the challenges of our own time are simply its latest chapter. Understanding where law came from won't tell us exactly where it's going, but it gives us the perspective to help shape what comes next.

End of Chapter Discussion Questions

Chapter 1: Was the shift from unwritten custom to written law truly progress, or a trade-off?

It was both, and treating it as pure progress misses what happened. Written law brought real gains. It gave people a fixed reference they could appeal to, ended the uncertainty of relying on fallible memories, and let justice be administered consistently across large territories. But something was lost too. Oral custom was flexible, able to adapt gradually as circumstances shifted, and it was genuinely the community's own, held collectively rather than imposed from above. Writing froze the law and, at the same time, handed rulers a powerful new tool for projecting authority over ordinary people. The same technology that made law knowable also made it an instrument of centralized power. So societies gained consistency, permanence, and scale, and they traded away flexibility, communal ownership of the law, and a certain protection against domination by the state. Whether that was worth it depends on what you value, and the honest answer is that large, complex societies probably couldn't function without written law, even as they lost something real in adopting it.

Chapter 2: Why did early societies root their laws in the divine, and what does a system gain and lose by claiming its rules come from beyond human judgment?

Early societies rooted law in the divine because it solved the enforcement problem in a world without police. If a rule comes from a mortal, people can ask why they should obey it and defy it if they think they can get away with it. If it comes from the gods, defiance risks supernatural punishment that no one can escape, a far more frightening prospect. Divine authority also gave law a permanence and weight that human rules couldn't match, placing it beyond ordinary challenge.

What a system gains from this is powerful, self-enforcing authority and stability. What it loses is the ability to openly revise its law. If the rules come from God, changing them means contradicting God, which makes reform difficult and can lock in injustices that outlive the circumstances that produced them. Divine authority buys obedience and stability at the cost of flexibility and honest self-correction.

Chapter 3: Can a legal system guard against the weaknesses of both popular judgment and rule by experts, or must it finally place its trust somewhere?

Every system must finally place its trust somewhere, but the best ones spread that trust across multiple points rather than concentrating it in one. Athens trusted the people entirely, and the people killed Socrates. Plato wanted to trust the wise, but couldn't say who they were or what would stop them from becoming tyrants. Both pure democracy and pure rule by experts fail because both concentrate ultimate trust in a single place. Modern legal systems try to escape this trap not by finding a perfect trustee but by dividing power and creating checks, mixing popular input through elections and juries with expert judgment through professional judges, and binding both to written constitutions that limit what either can do. This doesn't eliminate the risk. A system can still go wrong at every level.

But by refusing to place all its trust in any single actor, and by making each part answerable to the others, it reduces the chance that a single failure of judgment, whether by the crowd or by the experts, produces catastrophe. The trust is still there, but it's distributed rather than concentrated, and distribution is the closest thing we have to a safeguard.

Chapter 4: Is there something valuable in the Roman model of law developed by expert jurists, or does it place too much power in an unelected elite?

Both are true, and the tension is real. The Roman model had important strengths: law developed by expert jurists produced legal concepts of remarkable precision, consistency, and durability. Deep legal expertise often creates better legal doctrine than legislation shaped by short-term political pressures. But the danger is that unelected experts may reflect the values and interests of their own class rather than those of society. Modern legal systems try to balance these competing concerns by having democratically elected legislatures make the fundamental laws while judges and legal experts interpret and refine them. This combines expert legal reasoning with democratic legitimacy, though the balance remains an ongoing debate.

Chapter 5: If a legal system that openly ranks people can still function and last, are a legal order's fairness and its stability separate questions?

Largely, yes, and that's an uncomfortable truth. The traditions in this chapter built inequality directly into their laws, ranking people by caste or class, and they functioned and endured for centuries. This shows that a legal system's ability to last doesn't depend on its being fair. What stability actually requires is that a system be predictable, that it be accepted by enough of the population, especially the powerful, and that it deliver enough order to be preferable to chaos. A deeply unjust system can meet all these conditions, particularly if those it disadvantages lack the power to resist and if the surrounding culture treats the hierarchy as natural and right. So fairness and stability are separate questions. But not entirely separate. Systems that treat people unjustly generate resentment, and over long enough spans that resentment can become a source of instability, as the eventual overturning of caste and class systems suggests. Injustice may be compatible with stability in the short and medium term while quietly undermining it in the long run. The two questions are distinct, but they're connected at the edges.

Chapter 6: Could the absence of a single dominant legal authority in medieval Europe have been a strength rather than a weakness?

It may well have been, and this is one of the more surprising lessons of legal history. We instinctively assume that a unified legal system with one clear source of authority is better, cleaner, more rational. Yet medieval Europe's messy competition among rival legal orders, canon law, feudal law, royal law, town law, and merchant law, all operating at once and constantly jostling against one another, may have produced the very ideas about limited power that we most value. When multiple authorities compete, none can easily become absolute, because each is checked by the others. The Church limited kings, kings limited the Church, and both had to reckon with feudal lords, towns, and customary rights. Out of this competition grew the practical experience of power that was always contested and never total, and from that experience grew ideas about the rule of law and the limits of authority. A single dominant legal authority, by contrast, faces no such check and can more easily slide toward absolutism. This suggests that concentrating all legal authority in one place, however tidy, may be less protective of liberty than a more fragmented arrangement in which power must always contend with rival power.

Chapter 7: How can a legal system hold together a belief in unchanging divine law with the reality that humans must constantly interpret and apply it?

It does so by distinguishing between divine revelation and human interpretation. In the Islamic tradition, the Quran and the example of the Prophet are regarded as fixed and unchanging, while deriving detailed legal rules from them is the work of qualified scholars. This allows the foundation to remain constant even as its application adapts to new circumstances. The existence of multiple schools of jurisprudence reflects the understanding that sincere scholars can reach different, yet legitimate, conclusions from the same sources. Rather than weakening the system, this balance gives it both stability and flexibility. A sacred foundation provides enduring authority, while human interpretation allows the law to respond thoughtfully to changing societies and new legal questions.

Chapter 8: Can any legal system fully resolve the tension between consistency and fairness, or is something like equity a permanent feature?

Something like equity is a permanent feature, because the tension it addresses can't be designed away. The problem is built into the nature of rules themselves. Rules must be general to provide consistency, treating like cases alike and letting people know in advance where they stand. But general rules, applied to the endless variety of real situations, will sometimes produce results that are unjust in the particular case, because no rule can anticipate every circumstance. English law discovered this the hard way and grew a whole second body of law, equity, to correct the rigidity of the common law.

The deeper idea is that any system built entirely on firm rules will eventually generate unfair outcomes, and any system that always bends the rules to fit the circumstances will lose the consistency and predictability that make law valuable in the first place. So no system can fully resolve the tension. It can only manage it, keeping some mechanism, whether called equity, judicial discretion, or something else, that allows the rigidity of rules to yield to fairness when the result would otherwise be intolerable. The escape valve is permanent because the pressure it relieves is permanent.

Chapter 9: Was the contradiction between proclaiming universal rights and denying them to many a betrayal, or did it plant a standard that could later challenge those exclusions?

It was both a betrayal and a planted standard, and the two aren't mutually exclusive. The contradiction was real and inexcusable. Societies that declared all people to possess natural rights while holding people in slavery and excluding many from political life were guilty of a profound hypocrisy, and the people they wronged suffered no less for the fine words in the founding documents. To call it merely a stage in progress would insult those who bore the cost. And yet the act of proclaiming universal principles had consequences the proclaimers didn't fully intend or control. Once you declare that all people possess rights by virtue of their humanity, you've stated a standard that your own exclusions plainly violate, and that standard becomes available to anyone who wants to challenge those exclusions. Later movements to abolish slavery and extend rights did exactly this, holding societies to the universal principles they'd already proclaimed and demanding they live up to their own stated ideals. So the contradiction was genuinely a betrayal in its own time, and the proclaimed ideals genuinely became a weapon against the injustices they'd coexisted with. What this tells us is that the ideals a legal system proclaims matter even when it fails to honor them, because those ideals can outlast the failures and become the ground on which the failures are eventually overturned.

Chapter 10: Can law, historically slow and national, keep pace with challenges that are fast-moving and global, or must we rethink how law is made?

The honest answer is that traditional law, as it has worked for most of history, probably can't keep pace on its own, and some rethinking is unavoidable. Law has always moved slowly, and that slowness was often a virtue, allowing careful deliberation and letting rules develop through accumulated experience. Law has also been overwhelmingly national, made and enforced within the boundaries of individual states. Challenges like artificial intelligence break both of these assumptions at once. They develop faster than deliberative lawmaking can respond, and they cross borders freely, escaping the reach of any single nation's law. Meeting them will likely require new approaches: faster and more adaptive forms of regulation that can be updated as technology changes rather than fixed in slow-moving statutes, and greater cooperation and coordination among nations to address problems that no country can handle alone. What a legal system built for such a world might look like is still being worked out, but it would probably need to be more flexible, more international, and more capable of rapid adjustment than the largely national and slow-moving law we've inherited. The alternative, law that consistently arrives years after the problems it's meant to address and stops at borders the problems ignore, would leave some of the most consequential developments of our age effectively ungoverned.

A General Timeline of Legal History

Law grew across thousands of years, in different places, shaped by the needs and beliefs of the people who built it. What follows is a walk through the major moments in that long story, from the first stirrings of custom in prehistoric communities to the legal challenges we face today. The gaps between these moments are often enormous, and the developments rarely moved in a straight line, but together they trace how humanity learned to govern itself through law.

Before roughly 3000 BCE, the age of unwritten law. For the overwhelming majority of human existence, there was no writing, and so there was no written law. People lived under custom instead, rules held in memory and passed from one generation to the next through storytelling, ritual, and daily instruction. Disputes were settled by kin groups negotiating with one another, by respected elders mediating between the parties, and by the threat of revenge that hung over anyone who wronged another. Religion gave these rules their authority, since custom was understood to come from the gods or the ancestors rather than from mere mortals. This oral law governed human life for tens of thousands of years, and it worked, maintaining order in societies that had no police, no courts, and no judges in any sense we'd recognize. It was flexible and communal, but it depended entirely on memory, which meant it could drift and could be manipulated by whoever the community trusted to remember it.

Around 2100 BCE, the Code of Ur-Nammu. The oldest written law code that survives comes from the Sumerian city of Ur, and it predates its more famous successor by roughly three and a half centuries. Composed under King Ur-Nammu or his son, it opens with the ruler presenting himself as the protector of the weak against the strong, a pose that would echo through ancient law for two thousand years. Its most striking feature is that it settled many physical injuries with payments of silver rather than with retaliation, showing that even the very earliest written law could take a measured approach that some later codes abandoned.

Around 1750 BCE, the Code of Hammurabi. In Babylon, King Hammurabi had nearly three hundred laws carved onto a towering pillar of black stone and set up in public for all to see. This is the most complete legal document to survive from the ancient Near East, and it's famous for the principle of retribution in kind, the eye for an eye. But its deeper lesson is that the eye for an eye applied only between social equals. The code divided people into classes and prescribed sharply different penalties depending on the rank of the victim, openly building inequality into the very structure of justice. For all that, by publishing fixed penalties it made the consequences of actions predictable, a real step toward the rule of law even within a deeply unequal system.

Around 1650 to 1500 BCE, the Hittite Laws. Among the Hittites of Anatolia, a different philosophy took hold. Where Hammurabi leaned on physical retaliation, Hittite law relied far more on compensation and restitution, requiring wrongdoers to repair the harm rather than suffer matching injury. Remarkably, some of the Hittite legal texts record their own history of reform, explicitly noting that a punishment used to be harsher and has now been reduced. Few documents from the ancient world let us watch a legal system deliberately softening itself over time, with the old rule and the new one set side by side.

The centuries around 1200 BCE and after, Mosaic Law. The laws attributed to Moses, preserved in the Hebrew Bible, came from a small nation that never rivaled the great empires in power, yet their influence would eventually outstrip them all. Framed not as the work of a king but as law given directly by God, and bound up with a covenant between God and the people of Israel, Mosaic Law joined religious duty and social ethics into a single fabric. It carried a strong and repeated concern for the poor, the widow, the orphan, and the foreigner, and it included radical provisions like the Jubilee, meant to prevent permanent poverty. Through Judaism, Christianity, and Islam, it reached across continents and became woven into the ethical foundations of Western civilization.

Around 621 BCE, the laws of Draco. Athens took its first step out of aristocratic secrecy when a lawgiver named Draco wrote down the city's laws and made them public. Putting the law in writing was genuinely important, since it took the law out of the exclusive control of the noble families who alone had known it. But Draco's penalties were so brutally severe, prescribing death for even minor offenses, that his name gave us the word "draconian." His harsh code didn't calm Athens. It deepened the city's troubles.

Around 594 BCE, the reforms of Solon. With Athens sliding toward civil war, Solon was given extraordinary power to remake its laws, and he used it to become one of the founding figures of Western law. He canceled crushing debts, freed those who had been enslaved for debt, and abolished debt bondage entirely, lifting an enormous weight from the poor. He swept away nearly all of Draco's brutal penalties and replaced them with punishments that fit the offense. He opened political participation beyond the aristocracy and allowed any citizen to bring a case on behalf of someone wronged, planting the seed of the idea that a wrong against one member of the community concerns the whole community.

Around 450 BCE, the Twelve Tables. In Rome, the ordinary citizens, the plebeians, finally won their long struggle to have the law written down, ending the patrician monopoly on legal knowledge. The result was the Twelve Tables, inscribed and displayed publicly in the Forum, and they became the honored foundation of all later Roman law. Roman schoolchildren memorized them for centuries. More than any particular rule, they established the principle that all Romans, whatever their class, were subject to a common and publicly known law.

The fifth and fourth centuries BCE, Greek legal thought. This was the age when the Greeks became the first people to ask, systematically and philosophically, what law actually is. Athens put justice directly in the hands of enormous citizen juries, sometimes numbering in the hundreds or thousands, chosen by lot and voting by secret ballot without lawyers or judges to guide them. That same system condemned Socrates to death in 399 BCE, a permanent reminder that popular justice can go terribly wrong. Plato, shaped by his teacher's death, distrusted democracy and imagined rule by philosopher-kings, while his student Aristotle argued powerfully that law, being reason free from passion, should govern rather than any individual. Alongside them ran the idea of natural law, a higher justice grounded in nature and reason that stands above the laws of any particular city.

The centuries of the Roman Republic and Empire, the age of the jurists. Rome's lasting gift to law was to turn it into a working system and a genuine science. A distinctive class of legal experts, the jurists, developed Roman law not mainly through legislation but through expert interpretation, giving authoritative opinions on legal questions and reasoning carefully from established principles to handle new problems. They worked out concepts of extraordinary precision, distinguishing ownership from possession, analyzing the many kinds of contracts, and building a law of wrongful harm on the foundation of fault. In 212 CE, the emperor Caracalla extended citizenship to nearly all free inhabitants of the empire, making Roman law the common law of a vast population. Roman jurists approached legal questions systematically, comparing cases, refining definitions, and striving for logical consistency rather than simply issuing isolated decisions. Their methods became the foundation of civil law traditions and continue to influence legal education, judicial reasoning, and legal systems across much of the world today.

527 to 565 CE, Justinian's compilation. By the time the emperor Justinian reigned in the surviving eastern empire, Roman law had grown into a sprawling, contradictory mass of material accumulated over a thousand years. Justinian ordered a commission to gather it all, resolve its contradictions, and organize it into a coherent whole. The result, later called the Corpus Juris Civilis, preserved the essence of Roman legal science and became the vehicle through which it reached the modern world. Rediscovered in medieval Europe centuries later, it became the foundation of the civil law tradition that governs much of the world today.

The seventh century CE and after, the rise of Islamic law. With the birth of Islam came a comprehensive system of law understood as the expression of God's will for how human beings should live. Islamic law drew its authority from the Quran and from the recorded example of the Prophet Muhammad, and Muslim scholars developed it into a sophisticated legal science through methods including consensus and analogical reasoning. Four major schools of Sunni jurisprudence emerged, each recognizing the others as legitimate, an acceptance of reasoned diversity within a shared framework. Islamic commercial law, with its prohibition of interest and its concern for fairness, developed instruments that helped drive the flourishing trade of the medieval Muslim world and influenced commercial practice in Europe.

The medieval centuries in Europe, overlapping legal orders. After the western Roman Empire fell, Europe had no single legal authority but instead a patchwork of competing systems operating at once. Canon law, the law of the Catholic Church, reached across all of Western Christendom and governed matters like marriage that touched everyone's life. Feudal law organized society around relationships of loyalty and the holding of land in exchange for service, binding lords, vassals, and serfs in chains of mutual obligation. Kings, towns, and merchants each had their own law as well. This messy competition among rival authorities, in which no single power could easily become absolute, may have helped produce the very ideas about limited power that the West came to value most.

1215, Magna Carta. In a meadow beside the Thames, rebellious English barons forced King John to accept limits on his own power. Most of the Great Charter dealt with the specific feudal grievances of its time, but a few of its provisions expressed principles of lasting importance, declaring that even the king could not imprison or dispossess a free man arbitrarily, and that justice would not be sold, denied, or delayed. Reinterpreted and reissued over the centuries, Magna Carta grew into a great symbol of the principle that governmental power is limited by law and that even the highest authority must operate within legal bounds.

The twelfth century and after, the common law. In England, the medieval kings, and especially Henry II, built up a system of royal justice that became the foundation of the common law. Traveling royal judges carried the king's justice throughout the kingdom, and the law they applied became common to the whole realm rather than a patchwork of local customs. The common law developed case by case through the decisions of judges, with past decisions serving as precedents for future ones under the principle of stare decisis. Alongside it grew equity, a separate body of law administered by the Court of Chancery to provide fairness where the rigid common law fell short.

The seventeenth and eighteenth centuries, the age of revolution. These two centuries transformed the understanding of law and government more than any period since ancient Greece. Philosophers including Hobbes, Locke, and Rousseau developed theories of the social contract, arguing that government derives its authority from the consent of the governed and exists to serve the people rather than to rule them by divine right. England's Bill of Rights in 1689 secured constitutional limits on royal power. The United States Constitution built a government on the separation of powers, checks and balances, and the protection of rights. The French Revolution proclaimed the Declaration of the Rights of Man and produced the Napoleonic Code, a model of comprehensive codification that shaped the civil law world. Running through it all was natural rights theory, the idea that people possess rights simply by being human.

The twentieth century, international law and human rights. The modern age saw the growth of law reaching beyond the boundaries of individual nations. International law developed to govern relations among sovereign states, and after the Second World War the United Nations was established to maintain peace and promote cooperation. In 1948, the Universal Declaration of Human Rights proclaimed a broad range of rights held to belong to all human beings everywhere, giving new form to the long tradition of ideas about natural law and natural rights. International criminal justice emerged as well, holding individuals accountable for the gravest crimes through the post-war tribunals and, later, the permanent International Criminal Court.

The present and the road ahead. Today most of the world is governed by one of the two great traditions we've traced, the civil law descended from Rome or the common law born in England, while international and human rights law reach across their borders. And law now faces challenges unlike any before it. Digital technology has created new questions about data, privacy, and activity conducted online. Artificial intelligence is developing far faster than deliberative lawmaking has ever moved. The interconnection of a globalized world raises hard questions about which nation's law applies when everything crosses borders. Law has always been a relatively slow and largely national response to human problems, and whether it can keep pace with challenges that are both fast-moving and global is the open question of our time. The story that began on a Babylonian stone is still being written.

Key Terms and Definitions

- **Analogical reasoning (qiyas)** - A method in Islamic jurisprudence of extending established legal rules to new situations by reasoning from an existing rule that governs a similar case.
- **Arthashastra** - An ancient Indian treatise on statecraft, government, and law attributed to Kautilya, treating law as an instrument of royal power and practical governance.
- **Awilum** - The class of free men of full legal standing and property in Babylonian society under Hammurabi's Code, entitled to the fullest legal protections.
- **Bill of Rights (English)** - The 1689 English constitutional document that limited royal power, secured the role of Parliament, and addressed certain rights and liberties.
- **Bill of Rights (U.S.)** - The first ten amendments to the United States Constitution, protecting specified individual rights and liberties against governmental infringement.
- **Blood feud** - A cycle of retaliatory violence between kin groups, in which a wrong done by one group provokes revenge by the other, sometimes lasting for generations.
- **Bridewealth** - The transfer of goods from a groom's family to a bride's family in many early societies, functioning as a legal instrument binding the two families in mutual obligation.
- **Canon law** - The body of law of the Catholic Church, governing matters such as marriage, clergy, and various moral offenses, and applying across all of medieval Western Christendom.
- **Checks and balances** - A system in which each branch of government is given powers to restrain the others, reinforcing the separation of powers and guarding against the abuse of power.
- **Civil law tradition** - The legal tradition descended from Roman law, characterized by reliance on comprehensive written codes as the primary source of law, governing continental Europe, Latin America, and much of the world.
- **Code of Hammurabi** - The comprehensive Babylonian law code of around 1750 BCE, known for its class-based penalties and its use of retribution in kind.
- **Code of Ur-Nammu** - The oldest surviving written law code, dating to around 2100 BCE in the Sumerian city of Ur, notable for its reliance on monetary compensation for injuries.
- **Common law** - The legal tradition originating in medieval England, developed through judicial decisions and precedent, and spread to many nations of English legal heritage.
- **Common law (as "common")** - Law that applies commonly throughout an entire kingdom, as opposed to the varied local and customary laws that previously governed different regions.
- **Confucianism** - The Chinese tradition of thought holding that social order is best achieved through morality, virtue, and proper relationships rather than through law and punishment.
- **Consensus (ijma)** - The agreement of qualified scholars, or of the community, on a point of law, recognized as a source of authority in Islamic jurisprudence.
- **Constitutio Antoniniana** - The edict issued by the emperor Caracalla in 212 CE granting Roman citizenship to nearly all free inhabitants of the empire.

- **Corpus Juris Civilis** - The comprehensive compilation of Roman law produced under the emperor Justinian in the sixth century CE, which transmitted Roman legal science to later ages.
- **Corrective justice** - Aristotle's category of justice concerned with righting wrongs and restoring a fair balance when one person has wronged another.
- **Court of Chancery** - The English court that administered equity, providing relief based on fairness and conscience where the common law fell short.
- **Covenant** - In the Mosaic tradition, the binding agreement between God and the people of Israel, of which the law was understood to be the terms.
- **Decretum** - The twelfth-century compilation and systematic analysis of canon law produced by the scholar Gratian, which became foundational to the study of canon law.
- **Dharma** - A central concept in Indian thought encompassing law, duty, righteousness, and proper order, referring to the moral and social duties appropriate to a person's place and situation.
- **Digest (Pandects)** - The part of Justinian's compilation consisting of extracts from the writings of the classical Roman jurists, preserving the heart of Roman legal science.
- **Distributive justice** - Aristotle's category of justice concerned with the fair distribution of goods, honors, and resources among the members of a community.
- **Dominium** - The Roman concept of full and absolute ownership, the most complete right a person could have over property, distinct from mere possession.
- **Draconian** - Excessively harsh or severe, derived from the name of Draco, whose early Athenian laws prescribed death for a wide range of offenses.
- **Due process** - The principle that a person may not be deprived of life, liberty, or property except through proper legal procedures, with roots in Magna Carta.
- **Equity** - A body of law that developed in England alongside the common law, concerned with fairness in the particular case and providing remedies where the common law was inadequate.
- **Feudalism** - The medieval social, political, and economic system built around relationships of personal loyalty and the holding of land in exchange for service.
- **Fief** - Land granted by a lord to a vassal in the feudal system, held on condition of fulfilling the obligations owed to the lord.
- **General will** - Rousseau's concept of the collective will of the people directed toward the common good, held to be the basis of legitimate law and government.
- **Glorious Revolution** - The events surrounding the change of English monarchs in 1688 and 1689, accompanied by the establishment of constitutional principles limiting royal power.
- **Griot** - A West African specialist who served as a living archive of history, genealogy, and law in societies relying on oral tradition.
- **Hadith** - The recorded traditions concerning the sayings, actions, and approvals of the Prophet Muhammad, a primary source of Islamic law second only to the Quran.
- **Ius civile** - The civil law of Rome, which in the early period applied only to Roman citizens and governed their relationships and transactions.
- **Ius gentium** - The Roman "law of nations," applied in dealings involving non-citizens and based on principles regarded as common to all peoples.
- **Jubilee** - In Mosaic law, a year occurring every fifty years in which sold land was to return to its original families and Israelites in bondage were to be freed.
- **Jury** - A group of ordinary people who decide questions of fact in legal cases, an institution that became a distinctive feature of the common law tradition.

- **Justinian** - The Byzantine emperor who reigned from 527 to 565 CE and commissioned the great compilation of Roman law known as the Corpus Juris Civilis.
- **Kleroterion** - A stone device used in ancient Athens to randomly select jurors, designed to prevent tampering with the composition of juries.
- **Klepsydra** - A water clock used in Athenian courts to allot each side in a trial a fixed and equal amount of speaking time.
- **Legalism** - The Chinese school of thought holding that social order can be achieved only through strict laws, clear rewards and punishments, and firm state authority.
- **Lex Aquilia** - A Roman statute concerning wrongful damage to property, which the jurists interpreted and extended into a foundation for the law of wrongful harm.
- **Lex talionis** - The law of retaliation, the principle that a punishment should exactly match the offense, expressed in the phrase "an eye for an eye."
- **Logographer** - A professional speechwriter in ancient Athens who composed courtroom speeches for litigants to deliver as their own.
- **Ma'at** - The ancient Egyptian concept of truth, justice, balance, and cosmic order, understood as the principle that law and just conduct were meant to uphold.
- **Magna Carta** - The "Great Charter" of 1215, in which the English king accepted limits on his power, and which came to symbolize the principle that even the ruler is subject to law.
- **Manusmriti (Laws of Manu)** - An important ancient Indian legal and religious text that tied legal and social obligations closely to the hierarchy of caste.
- **Mosaic Law** - The body of law attributed to Moses in the Hebrew Bible, framed as given by God, and profoundly influential on Western legal and moral thought.
- **Mufti** - A qualified Islamic scholar who gives authoritative legal opinions, known as fatwas, on points of law.
- **Mushkenum** - An intermediate class of commoners or dependents in Babylonian society under Hammurabi's Code, ranking below the free awilum.
- **Napoleonic Code** - The comprehensive codification of French civil law enacted under Napoleon, which became a highly influential model for legal codification in the civil law tradition.
- **Natural law** - The idea of a higher law, grounded in nature or reason, that stands above human-made law and against which human laws can be measured.
- **Natural rights** - Rights that individuals are held to possess by nature, prior to and independent of government, which government and law ought to respect and protect.
- **Nomos** - The Greek term for law, custom, or convention, the rules that particular human societies make, contrasted with physis, or nature.
- **Oral tradition** - The transmission of law and custom through memory and speech rather than writing, characteristic of pre-literate societies.
- **Ordeal** - A method of determining guilt or innocence by subjecting an accused person to a physical test, based on the belief that the divine would protect the innocent.
- **Paterfamilias** - The male head of a household in Roman society, holding extensive legal power over his wife, children, and slaves.
- **Peace of Westphalia** - The seventeenth-century settlement often associated with the development of the modern system of sovereign states.
- **Physis** - The Greek term for nature, the way things really are independent of human choice, contrasted with nomos, or human convention.
- **Popular sovereignty** - The principle that the people are the ultimate source of legitimate political authority, emphasized in the thought of Rousseau.

- **Possession** - The actual physical control of a thing, distinct in Roman law from ownership, which is the legal right to a thing.
- **Precedent** - A past judicial decision that serves as authority for deciding later cases involving similar circumstances, central to the common law tradition.
- **Qadi** - The Islamic judge responsible for hearing cases, applying Islamic law, and rendering judgments in the courts.
- **Quran** - The holy book of Islam, understood by Muslims as the revealed word of God, and the highest and foundational source of Islamic law.
- **Restitution** - The settling of wrongs by the payment of goods or compensation rather than by retaliation, an early alternative to revenge.
- **Riba** - Interest or usury, prohibited in Islamic commercial law on the ground that it involves unjust gain, leading to the development of alternative financial arrangements.
- **Rule of law** - The principle that law, rather than the arbitrary will of individuals, should govern, and that even rulers are subject to the law.
- **Seisachtheia** - Solon's reform in ancient Athens, the "shaking off of burdens," which canceled debts and freed those enslaved for debt.
- **Separation of powers** - The division of governmental power among distinct branches, legislative, executive, and judicial, to prevent the concentration of power.
- **Serf** - A peasant in the feudal system who was bound to the land and owed labor and dues to the lord, holding a status of unfreedom distinct from slavery.
- **Sharia** - The divine law of Islam, God's guidance for how human beings should live, encompassing the comprehensive body of Islamic law.
- **Social contract** - The idea that government arises from, or can be understood as based on, an agreement among people, developed by Hobbes, Locke, and Rousseau.
- **Stare decisis** - The principle of standing by decided cases, requiring courts to follow the precedents established in earlier decisions.
- **State of nature** - The imagined condition without government used by social contract theorists to explain the origin and purpose of government.
- **Sunnah** - The example of the Prophet Muhammad, his sayings, actions, and approvals, recorded in the Hadith and serving as a source of Islamic law.
- **Trust** - An arrangement developed by equity in which property is held by one person for the benefit of another, an enduring institution in common law systems.
- **Twelve Tables** - The first written code of Roman law, dating to around 450 BCE, which made the law public and became the honored foundation of Roman law.
- **Universal Declaration of Human Rights** - The 1948 document adopted by the United Nations proclaiming a broad range of fundamental rights held to belong to all human beings.
- **Vassal** - A person in the feudal system who held land from a lord in exchange for service and loyalty, bound to the lord by mutual obligation.
- **Wergild** - The "man-price" in early Germanic law, the compensation owed for killing a person, set according to the person's rank and status.
- **Writ** - A formal written order used in the developing common law to initiate a legal action in the royal courts, with different writs for different kinds of claims.

References & Recommended Readings

Works Cited

Aristotle. (1998). *Politics* (C. D. C. Reeve, Trans.). Hackett Publishing. (Original work published c. 350 BCE)

Aristotle. (2000). *Nicomachean ethics* (R. Crisp, Trans.). Cambridge University Press. (Original work published c. 350 BCE)

Berman, H. J. (1983). *Law and revolution: The formation of the Western legal tradition.* Harvard University Press.

Bix, B. H. (2019). *Jurisprudence: Theory and context* (8th ed.). Sweet & Maxwell.

Cartledge, P. (2016). *Democracy: A life.* Oxford University Press.

Coulson, N. J. (2011). *A history of Islamic law.* Edinburgh University Press.

Driver, G. R., & Miles, J. C. (1952). *The Babylonian laws* (Vols. 1–2). Oxford University Press.

Glenn, H. P. (2014). *Legal traditions of the world: Sustainable diversity in law* (5th ed.). Oxford University Press.

Hallaq, W. B. (2009). *An introduction to Islamic law.* Cambridge University Press.

Hobbes, T. (1996). *Leviathan* (R. Tuck, Ed.). Cambridge University Press. (Original work published 1651)

Holt, J. C. (2015). *Magna Carta* (3rd ed.). Cambridge University Press.

Kelly, J. M. (1992). *A short history of Western legal theory.* Oxford University Press.

Locke, J. (1988). *Two treatises of government* (P. Laslett, Ed.). Cambridge University Press. (Original work published 1689)

Roebuck, D. (2001). *Ancient Greek arbitration.* Holo Books.

Rousseau, J.-J. (1997). *The social contract and other later political writings* (V. Gourevitch, Ed. & Trans.). Cambridge University Press. (Original work published 1762)

Sarat, A., & Kearns, T. R. (Eds.). (1994). *The rhetoric of law.* University of Michigan Press.

Stein, P. (1999). *Roman law in European history.* Cambridge University Press.

Tamanaha, B. Z. (2004). *On the rule of law: History, politics, theory.* Cambridge University Press.

Van Caenegem, R. C. (1988). *The birth of the English common law* (2nd ed.). Cambridge University Press.

VerSteeg, R. (2002). *Law in the ancient world.* Carolina Academic Press.

Watson, A. (1995). *The spirit of Roman law*. University of Georgia Press.

Westbrook, R. (Ed.). (2003). *A history of ancient Near Eastern law* (Vols. 1–2). Brill.

Wolff, H. J. (1951). *Roman law: An historical introduction*. University of Oklahoma Press.

Zweigert, K., & Kötz, H. (1998). *An introduction to comparative law* (T. Weir, Trans., 3rd ed.). Oxford University Press.

References & Recommended Readings

Berman, H. J. (1983). *Law and revolution: The formation of the Western legal tradition*. Harvard University Press.

- A sweeping account of how the Western legal tradition took shape in the medieval period. If you read only one deeper work after this book, this is a strong choice for understanding how law and Western civilization grew together.

Glenn, H. P. (2014). *Legal traditions of the world: Sustainable diversity in law* (5th ed.). Oxford University Press.

- The best single book for seeing the world's legal traditions side by side rather than through a Western lens alone.

Westbrook, R. (Ed.). (2003). *A history of ancient Near Eastern law* (Vols. 1–2). Brill.

- The definitive scholarly reference on the earliest legal systems, covering the codes we examined and many more in authoritative detail. Dense, but unmatched for anyone wanting to go deep on ancient law.

Stein, P. (1999). *Roman law in European history*. Cambridge University Press.

- A concise and readable account of how Roman law survived, revived, and shaped European legal systems across the centuries. It's an ideal next step for readers who found the chapter on Rome compelling.

Tamanaha, B. Z. (2004). *On the rule of law: History, politics, theory*. Cambridge University Press.

- Traces the idea of the rule of law from antiquity to the present with clarity and balance. Recommended for readers drawn to the recurring question, running through this whole book, of whether the powerful can truly be bound by law.